Igniting An Impassioned Prayer Life

How to Develop the Energized, Extended, and
Sustainable Life of Prayer You've Always Wanted

TOM STUART

Paul -
with thankfulness
for your amazing
kingdom work and
inspiration!
Tom   colossians 4:2

Dedication

To my loving wife and prayer partner, Susan.
Your faithful companionship in life's journey continually
sustains and inspires me to abide in Jesus' presence and trust
Him no matter where He leads.

Contents

Section III: Prayer Mandates

Section IV: Make Me a House of Prayer

Section V: Ministry of the Watchman/Intercessor

Section VI: Praying Prayers that Get Answers

Section VII: Overcoming Obstacles to Prayer

Acknowledgments

In the writing of this book I was aided by the wise input and faithful encouragement of three individuals without whom the task would have remained undone or woefully lacking.

First to my wife Susan: your love, prayers, and counsel have been like a lifeline to me. I deeply appreciate your patience in reading every word of every chapter as it was being written and giving me your constructive recommendations for improvement. Your life, so simply devoted to prayer and the presence of Jesus, is my ever-present source of inspiration.

I also want to express my gratefulness to Bonnie Newberg, a woman of the Word and faith-filled intercessor, who joyfully proofed and prayed over my manuscript. Your prayers and encouraging words were a gift from God, reassuring me that the task was worth finishing. Your infectious zeal for God and prayer quickens faith in all of us who are blessed to come in contact with you.

I **cannot say enough about my final editor, Julie Hawkinson**, except that without you my book would have been a difficult read. Your meticulous and insightful editorial input lifted the book to a level of readability heretofore not associated with my writing. Thank you for your perseverance in seeing the project through and encouraging me along the way! In the process I learned a lot about such things as grammar, sentence structure, and punctuation. Thank you.

To all those intercessors, too numerous to mention, with whom I have had the privilege over the years of laboring together in prayer: thank you for your companionship! Together we stormed heavens gates, filled early morning and evening watches, persevered through all-nighters, and spent weeks in prayer and fasting. Together we learned what it meant to be enrolled in Christ's school of prayer, kneeling at the feet of the Master. Thanks to each and every one of you from Way of the Cross, Bridgewood Community Church and Twin Cities House of Prayer! You know who you are and I will forever treasure my times of prayer with you!

Finally, I want to thank God my heavenly Father, Christ Jesus my Lord, and the Holy Spirit my counselor, for gracing me to finally see this book in print! Thank you for calling me out of darkness into your marvelous light, giving my life meaning and purpose, and empowering me to walk with You and pray prayers that get answer. Thank you for fulfilling my dream to share with others what you have shared with me about prayer. All glory, praise, and honor belong to You!

Introduction

Why another book on prayer with tens of thousands already in print? When it comes to prayer, I feel like the merchant in Jesus' parable who was "seeking fine pearls" (Matthew 13:45 NASB). I have spent most of my Christian life seeking pearls of wisdom for energizing and sustaining a vibrant prayer life. Ironically, after more than forty years, it has been just recently that the Lord has allowed me to discover an overall approach to prayer which I would consider that "one pearl of great price." Like the merchant Jesus spoke about, I have chosen to pay whatever price is necessary and do everything I can to call this "pearl" my own. As a result, this pearl has so revolutionized my prayer life that I am compelled to share the spiritual wealth it is bringing me with everyone I can. That is my reason for writing this book.

It must be stressed, as a foundational premise for this book, that igniting and fueling an impassioned prayer life is only possible through an utter dependence upon the Holy Spirit. Prayer that is not Spirit bred, Spirit led, and

Spirit fed, is in a word, dead. The Bible repeatedly emphasizes that our communication with God must be *in the Spirit*. The Apostle Paul urges us to "pray in the Spirit on all occasions" (Ephesians 6:18 NIV). Attentiveness to the spontaneity of the Spirit is absolutely necessary in prayer because it is through the Holy Spirit that revelation, faith, and God's power are all released (Zechariah 4:6). It is the Spirit that "helps us in our weakness," teaches how to pray, and, when necessary, even intercedes for us (Romans 8:26).

In a nutshell, my discovery to developing an impassioned prayer life has three essential ingredients: presence, structure and spontaneity, and mandates.

Sections I, II, and III of the book are dedicated to introducing you to these principles and helping you practically apply them in your prayer life. I am thoroughly convinced, from the Scriptures, my personal experience, and the testimony of others, that these are the three non-negotiables of vital prayer. Every person who embraces these practices as a regular daily priority, in utter dependence upon the Holy Spirit, will experience the energized, extended, and sustainable life of prayer they've always wanted.

Section IV: *Make Me a House of Prayer*, **begins with my personal testimony of a life changing prayer that God challenged me to pray.** It goes on to describe how we, both individually and corporately as a church, can fulfill Jesus' mandate that His church be a house of prayer for all nations. The last chapter in this section, *Making Your Church a House of Prayer*, lays out a very practical way in which a prayer-less church can be transformed into a praying church.

Section V profiles the prayer ministries of the watchman and intercessor. It is designed to help you clarify and give greater release to God's calling in your life with regard to prayer. It explains the Biblical foundation for intercession and applicable principles of how it works. The final chapter in this section (31), *Guidelines for Effective Intercession*, provides what arguably might be considered the most reliable and widely used approach to intercession introduced within the last fifty years. It clearly spells out practical ways in which to invite, yield to, hear from, and pray authoritatively in the Holy Spirit. People who follow these steps in their time of prayer never fail to experience the remarkable presence of God.

Sections VI and VII were written specifically for those who need encouragement to persevere in prayer. Check out the titles in these two sections. It might be where you need to begin in reading this book. Chapter 32, *Six Prayers God Always Answers* is taken from a familiar passage of Scripture you may never have realized contained such amazing promises. Chapter 37, *The Most Powerful Prayer You Can Pray* may also surprise you. This chapter originated as a blog post in 2010, and it has been the most Googled article I have ever written.

Maybe you have run into a major roadblock or detour in your praying. Section VII is designed to help you deal with some of these obstacles. It addresses false assumptions and silent delays, two hurdles every prayer warrior must clear on the way to answered prayer. It also outlines some practical things you can do in that waiting period between the ask and the answer. For those who feel like giving up on prayer, the last chapter of the book (43), *When All Else Fails, Let Jesus Pray*, may have been written just for you.

There you have it - an overview of my book meant to whet your appetite and help you navigate these pages to derive maximum benefit. It is my hope and prayer that the Holy Spirit will illuminate those portions of this book that you need to ignite His passion in you for His presence and a revitalized prayer life.

In humble expectation, Tom Stuart

1

The Life of Jesus - Our Call to Prayer

During the days of Jesus' life on earth, He offered up prayers and petitions with fervent cries and tears to the one who could save Him from death, and He was heard because of His reverent submission. Hebrews 5:7 NIV

The most compelling argument ever presented for cultivating a praying lifestyle is found in studying the life and teachings of Jesus. Jesus was both the quintessential pray-er and the world's unparalleled expert on prayer. There are well over 100 verses in the gospels that recount His personal prayer habits, His teachings on prayer and, thankfully, many of His actual prayers.

We know that His life was punctuated by prayer from the beginning of His ministry to the end, and He did it as naturally as breathing. He was praying when the Holy Spirit descended upon Him at His baptism in the Jordan River. He was praying with His last breath from the cross. He was wont to spend both late nights and early mornings in prayer. It was not unusual for Him to pull all-nighters when wrestling with weighty decisions like His choice of the twelve apostles (Luke 6:12-13).

During the day He was continually praying for the needs of the multitudes who pressed in upon Him or pausing simply to give thanks to His Heavenly Father for what He saw His Father doing. His communion with heaven was an ongoing dialogue, and the entirety of one of those many prayer conversations is recorded in John 17 as a model for the ages. One thing is readily evident in considering Jesus' life: prayer was a priority.

While Jesus' life demonstrated the importance of prayer, His teachings provided the practical how-tos. His prayer life was so remarkable that those closest to Him were compelled to ask Him to teach them how to pray. What followed is now considered the most comprehensive, yet succinct, teachings on prayer ever given. In what we commonly refer to as the Lord's Prayer, Jesus laid out a logical, sequential outline to use in praying for everything from heavenly and global concerns to local and personal needs (Matthew 6:1-13; Luke 11:1-4). But the scope of Jesus' teaching on prayer went way beyond what was contained in those five verses.

Jesus taught about prayer on many occasions. In fact, all four gospels contain different accounts of Jesus explaining ways in which to pray effectively. The Gospel of Matthew records Jesus emphasizing the importance of praying to the Father in secret, often coupled with fasting and giving (Matthew 6:1-8; 16-18). We also see Jesus teaching about the principles of binding and loosing, and the prayer of agreement (Matthew 18:18-19). In Mark we find Jesus exhorting His followers to "have faith in God" when praying, to profess out loud their belief, and to forgive anyone who has offended them (Mark 11:22-25). In Luke Jesus tells three different parables underscoring the importance of persistence when praying (Luke 11:5-8; 9-13; Luke 18:1-8). Furthermore in the gospel of John, Jesus explains in detail the importance of praying to the Father in His name (John 14:13-14; 15:16; 16:23-27).

In addition to all this, Jesus gave very specific instructions with regard to what to pray for. To name a few, He urged praying for blessing on our enemies, for harvest workers to be raised up, for protection from temptation, and for the Holy Spirit (Matthew 5:44 & 9:38; Matthew 26:20 & 41; Luke 11:13). Interestingly, His most urgent and dramatic call to prayer was for the nations of the world. When He cleansed the temple the week leading up to His death, He cried, "Is it not written: 'My house will be called a house of prayer for all nations. But you have made it 'a den of robbers'" (Mark 11:17 NIV).

Finally, and it is not without significance, the last appeal Jesus ever made was with regard to prayer. It was in essence a "deathbed request" uttered within the final 24 hours of His life, right before He was arrested and whisked away from His disciples in the garden of Gethsemane. Deathbed requests demand serious consideration and a resolve to see them fulfilled. It came in the midst of His agonizing in prayer over His impending crucifixion. At one point He took a break and went to His disciples, only to find them sleeping. It was then that He challenged them with this question - **"Couldn't you watch with me even one hour?"** It is a challenge that echoes down through the corridors of time to this very day, to every person who considers themselves a disciple (Matthew 26:40 NLT).

Jesus' emphasis on the critical importance of prayer is best underscored by His utter dependence upon it in His own life. The book of Hebrews gives us a behind the scenes glimpse. We are told that "During the days of Jesus' life on earth, He offered up prayers and petitions with fervent cries and tears to the one who could save Him from death, and He was heard because of His reverent submission" (Hebrews 5:7 NIV).

Considering Jesus' great dependence upon the Father in prayer, how much more dependent should we be? Considering the passion, urgency and consistency with which Jesus, the Son of God was required to pray, how much more are we? Considering His many teachings and urgings to pray, why do we delay?

For further meditation and application:

What things about the life and teachings of Jesus most motivate you to develop a similar life of prayer?

2

The Priority of Spiritual Habits

And He came to Nazareth, where He had been brought up. And as was His custom, He went to the synagogue on the Sabbath day, and He stood up to read. Luke 4:16 ESV

"As was His custom" – these are four simple words that communicate volumes. What does that phrase, applied to your life, tell everyone about you?

In many ways our customs, or habits, define us because they tell us what things give priority to our lives. The ideal is to establish regular practices and habits that impart energy, provide stability and/or add meaning to life. When consider daily routines – we think of our dietary habits, ways in which we keep informed and engage with media, and our exercise routines or the lack thereof. However the most important habits to establish in life are the spiritual ones.

Jesus was a creature of habit when it came to His spiritual life. He made a commitment to habitual daily, weekly, and even annual practices that nourished His personal relationship with His Heavenly Father. These practices also became the platform from which He launched a good portion of His ministry. Daily prayer, early in the morning or late at night, weekly engagement in worship and the Scriptures each Sabbath at the synagogue, and regular attendance at the annual feasts in Jerusalem were the benchmarks of His spiritual life.

If Jesus, fully God, yet fully man, made daily communion with God and weekly engagement in worship the priority in His life, how much more should we? Paul, following in Jesus' footsteps, began each week in the synagogue as well. *"As was Paul's custom,* he went to the synagogue service, and for three Sabbaths in a row he used the Scriptures to reason with the people" (Acts 17:2 NLT *emphasis added*).

Daniel and David were monsters of the faith when it came to their prayer habits. We are told that Daniel, even under the threat of death, ". . . prayed three times a day, *just as he had always done,* giving thanks to his God" (Daniel 6:10 NLT *emphasis added*). And David makes an incredible declaration of his habitual commitment: *"Seven times a day* I praise you for you righteous laws" (Psalm 119:164 NIV *emphasis added*).

What are your spiritual customs?

When I first became a Christian, I had godly mentors who in word and deed challenged me to incorporate key spiritual habits into my life. These have been the mainstay of my Christian life and relationship with God.

One was a "No Bible, No Breakfast" commitment. Years ago I made a decision to read through the entire Bible once each year for the rest of my life. Installments of that scripture journey continue to the present. They are the foundation of my day and the primary way in which God speaks to me. It has not always been easy and, like any commitment, has been tested. Sometimes my *No Bible, No Breakfast* maxim has turned into No *Bible, No Bedtime.*

Coupled with that has been a daily commitment to prayer. Typically the outline of prayer provided in the Lord's Prayer has been my guide. Logging a prayer journal has also been a huge help in keeping me on track. Yes, at times a busy schedule and unforeseen circumstances have derailed me, and I have missed some days. Even so, my habitual commitments to a Bible reading plan and prayer have always steered me back on track.

The other custom which, from my conversion, has been deeply ingrained in me is to make weekly church attendance and worship with the Body of Christ a priority, even when I am out of town. It has been concerning for me to read the national statistics and see anecdotal evidence even in my own church of less frequent church attendance by believers. Whereas in decades past, weekly Sunday attendance was the norm, we are now seeing church members attending only 2 or 3 times a month.

Spiritual habits are the responsibility of the individual. Bottom line: no one can attend church for you. No one can read your Bible for you. No one can commune with God in prayer for you. It is incumbent upon each of us as individuals to develop customs that will nurture our relationship with God.

For further meditation and application:

It might be beneficial for you to take some time to consider what might be said of your spiritual customs. Are they illustrative of your desire to know God better and to become more like His Son Jesus? If not, what changes is the Holy Spirit moving upon your heart to make?

3

The Call to Be With Him

He appointed twelve that they might be with him and that he might send them out to preach. Mark 3:14 NIV

The order in which Mark, the author of this gospel, describes Jesus' calling of His disciples is critically significant. Jesus' intention was that first they were to "be with" Him, to spend time in His presence, hang out together with Him, and get to know Him and His ways. Then and only then, when they had become immersed in His presence and shaped to faithfully represent His name and nature, would He send them out to preach. Although the task of going forth as His ambassadors was His ultimate purpose, Jesus' first calling to His disciples was that they might simply be with Him.

It reflects the priority Jesus placed throughout His earthly ministry on *being* preceding *doing* and the necessity of *doing* then flowing out of *being*. The spiritual journey of every disciple who is seeking to follow Jesus must always follow this pattern.

We are by nature, particularly in Western Culture, more preoccupied with doing than with being. Accomplishment, image, and the outer life all too often take precedence over nurturing authentic relationships and the inner life. Sadly we gravitate toward defining our identity more by our outer life and what we do than by our inner life and who we really are (our true self) in relationship with God. Nowhere does this become more evident than when circumstances limit or restrict us from accomplishing the things we are accustomed to doing. It is then that we can experience what the world terms an "identity crisis".

In kingdom of God parlance, an identity crisis is when God calls us to let go of everything in our lives in which we are seeking an identity (the false self) and choosing to find our identity in relationship to God.

What then does it mean as a disciple of Jesus Christ to answer this call to make being with Him the one great priority of our lives? Because Jesus is no longer upon the earth in bodily form, our relationship with Him has to be a spiritual one. For some that may seem a bit confusing if not problematic, in knowing how to proceed. But the principles and nuances of building a relationship with Jesus in the Spirit are essentially the same as when the early disciples were hanging out with Him when He was upon the earth in the flesh.

I don't know of any other way to describe it than to say that *being with* someone is spending time with them.

Jesus, himself modeled this *spiritual* "being with" as He nurtured His relationship with His Father. It was His custom to spend time with the Father as often as He could, and it took the form of prayer. Whether it was in the night or early morning hours in a solitary place or simply lifting His eyes, His heart, and His voice toward heaven in the midst of daily ministry demands, Jesus always found time to *be with* the Father. Sometimes it was expressed poignantly by nothing more than a wordless sigh. But no matter what form it took, or where it happened, or whether alone or with others, His heart and mind were directed toward heaven, and He was acknowledging His dependence upon the Father and the love they shared.

We must be very careful here not to gravitate toward a preconceived, limited, or stilted view of prayer. Paul, in writing to the Ephesians, emphasized the multifaceted nature of our communication with God through prayer by saying, "pray in the Spirit on all occasions with all kinds of prayers and requests" (Ephesians 6:18 NIV).

Just as lovers develop their own love language, so the disciple with his or her Lord will find unique and meaningful ways to communicate. The most important thing is "being with" one another and spending time together. That is the first calling and priority of every disciple of Jesus Christ.

For further meditation and application:

If you were to change one thing about your prayer life to enable you to more seriously answer this call, what should it be?

4

God's Presence – Our Priority in Prayer

You make known to me the path of life; in your presence there is fullness of joy; at your right hand are pleasures forevermore. Psalm 16:11 ESV

The singular truth about prayer that can most revolutionize a person's prayer life is this – the primary purpose of prayer is be in God's presence. When we make our aim, first and foremost, simply to enter into and experience God's presence, our understanding of prayer takes on transformative meaning. Prayer becomes a relationship more than a responsibility, a place more than a process, a delight more than a drudgery and an end more than a means.

The prayer life of Jesus and the way in which He related to His disciples illustrates this priority in prayer. In His own personal life, Jesus frequently sought a solitary place in which He could commune with His Father in prayer. On occasion He brought some of His disciples with Him, and the divine encounters He had with the Heavenly Father so impressed them that they finally asked Him to teach them to pray (Luke 11:1). His response is noteworthy. He began by encouraging them to seek out a relationship with the heavenly Father themselves, instructing them to pray "Father, hallowed be Thy name. . . ."

When Jesus chose the twelve, He established this same priority emphasizing that relationship precedes responsibility. We are told "He appointed twelve that they might be with him and that he might send them out to preach" (Mark 3:14 NIV). One cannot help but notice that His first concern and purpose was that they simply "be with him." That is Jesus' desire for each of us with regard to prayer – simply to spend time *with* Him.

One of the best verses in the Bible that embodies God's ultimate purpose for prayer, and intended blessings from it, is found in Psalm 16:11. It was penned by David who is singularly described as a man after God's own heart (Acts 13:22). "You make known to me the path of life; in your presence there is fullness of joy; at your right hand are pleasures forevermore." The promise embedded in this verse is that out of God's presence flows not only joy but also the revelation of His will, i.e. "the path of life." The wonder of this priority in prayer is that in God's presence His perspective and will are revealed, thus enabling us to pray by revelation for the things that are upon His heart. That in turn releases faith because "if we ask anything according to his will, he hears us. And if we know that he hears us—whatever we ask—we know that we have what we asked of him" (1 John 5:14-15 NIV).

Practically then, what does prayer look like when finding joy in the presence of Lord becomes our overarching desire? Here are several things that can help the pray-er seeking God's presence.

1. Recognize the unique pathway God has provided for you to commune with Him and follow it. Each person has an innately preferred way in which to enter into, and become aware of, the presence of the Lord. It may be through worship music, or Bible study, or nature, or liturgy, or activism, or contemplation, etc. It may be related to a specific time of day that works best for you such as early morning or late at night. It may be related to a specific place, indoors or out, where you find an intimate place to meet with Him. For more on this topic check out the book *Sacred Pathways* by Gary Thomas.

2. Begin with thanksgiving and praise. Nothing ushers us into the presence of the Lord more powerfully and releases His perspective more readily than thanksgiving. That is why we are frequently exhorted in the Bible to "enter his gates with thanksgiving and his courts with praise; give thanks to him and praise his name" (Psalm 100:4 NIV). It is good to recount the faithfulness of God in our lives and rehearse back to Him our thankfulness for that faithfulness.

3. Be sensitive to the conviction of the Holy Spirit and quick to acknowledge and repent of any sin. The blood of Jesus cleanses us from all unrighteousness and gives us bold confidence to enter into His presence (1 John 1:7, Hebrews 10:19). With open arms the waiting Father is always standing ready to welcome the prodigal home into His loving embrace.

4. Ask for and yield to the presence of the Holy Spirit. The Holy Spirit, third person of the Trinity, is the manifestation of God's presence on earth. Welcoming the Holy Spirit, who proceeds from the Father and the Son, is also welcoming them. It is He, the Comforter and Counselor, who takes what they are saying and doing and reveals them to us. "Likewise the Spirit helps us in our weakness. For we do not know what to pray for as we ought, but the Spirit himself intercedes for us with groanings too deep for words" (Romans 8:26 ESV).

5. Seek to silence the voice of self and Satan so that you can hear the voice of God. Distractive thoughts are often enemy number one whenever a person sets their heart to be in God's presence. There are ways to be proactive in silencing all the other interruptive and usurping voices. First take time to cast all the burdens you are carrying upon the Lord. He invites us to let Him be our burden bearer (Psalm 55:22; 1 Peter 5:7). Second, take authority over every demonic voice, silencing it in the mighty name of Jesus, believing "No weapon forged against you will prevail" (Isaiah 54:17 NIV). Third, keep a notepad nearby in which you can write down things you want to remember that come to mind and tend to pull you off track from seeking God. Finally, as you begin to delight yourself in the presence of the Lord and hear His voice, use that same means or a journal to capture the things He is revealing to you.

For further meditation and application:

What have you learned about experiencing God's presence in prayer? Are you daily putting these things into practice and making His presence the priority of your time in prayer?

5

What it Means to Pray With Jesus!

Couldn't you watch with Me even one hour?
Matthew 26:40 NLT

As we saw in chapter three, *The Call to Be With Him*, when Jesus initially called His disciples and us, His first and primary intention was, and always will remain, that we simply be *with* Him. The point was made that being with Him is expressed most naturally through relating to Him in prayer, just as He related to the Father.

The very last time Jesus was with His disciples, before He was crucified, He renewed that "be with" calling in a way that has been indelibly etched in the heart of every follower of Christ. Knowing He would no longer be with them in the natural, He was preparing them for a post-resurrection relationship with Him in the Spirit. One of the last things He said to Peter, James and John in the Garden of Gethsemane was "remain here and keep watch *with Me*" (Matthew 26:38 ESV *emphasis added*). He then moved further beyond them "about a stone's throw away" and, falling with

His face to the ground, He began praying with such fervency that "His sweat became like drops of blood."

When He arose from prayer, He came back to the three and found them sleeping. It was then that He said these oft-quoted and hauntingly powerful words "Couldn't you watch *with Me* even on hour?" (Matthew 26: 40 NLT *emphasis added*).

The two words that I want to give special consideration to in this meditation are "with Me." In the Gethsemane account in the book of Matthew we see in the space of three verses Jesus urging His disciples to watch and pray using the "with Me" reference two successive times, verses 38 and 39.

Prayer "with" Jesus is *the* critical distinguishing characteristic of Christian prayer in comparison to the prayers of all the other religious traditions. The very essence of prayer for followers of Christ is found in that simple phrase "with Me."

We must ask the question, "Where is Jesus right now?" The obvious answer is that "Jesus is in heaven." We are told in Paul's letter to the Ephesians that when God raised Christ Jesus from the dead, He "seated Him at His right hand in the heavenly realms far above all rule and authority and dominion and every title that can be given, not only in the present age but also in the one to come" (Ephesians 1:20-12 NIV).

The next question we must ask is "What is Jesus doing right now?" If we can fully grasp the answer to that question, it will change how we pray. **To put it succinctly, Jesus is still interceding.** The writer to Hebrews gives us an incredible insight into Jesus' present day activity when he says that Jesus "always lives to intercede for" those who come to God through Him (Hebrews 7:25 NIV).

Here is the bottom line: we have been invited, even urged, to watch and pray *with* Jesus. **To pray *with* Jesus means to pray with power and authority!** You see, Paul's description of Christ's ascension and seating in the heavenlies didn't stop there. The next verse in Ephesians says, "And God placed all things under His feet and appointed Him to be head over everything *for* the church, which is His body, the fullness of Him who fills everything in every way" (Ephesians 1:22-23 NIV *emphasis added*). Did you notice the word "for"? All this was "for" a praying church. And where are we invited to be as praying people? We are told in the next chapter "God raised us up with Christ and seated us *with Him* in the heavenly realms in Christ Jesus" (Ephesians 2:6 NIV). There is that phrase "with Him" again.

It is amazing to consider that the invitation to watch and pray with Him is an invitation to be seated with Him in a place of absolute authority. Praying from that place distinguishes us from all other types of pray-ers. We can pray with unshakable faith, and we can have confidence that we will get results. **Praying with the Master Pray-er guarantees success!**

If a master carpenter said to you "Come build a house with me," how do you think it would turn out? Undoubtedly the project would be a great success. If the master carpenter sent you to the lumber yard to get a certain type of building material that was needed and told you to say to the front desk, "The Master Carpenter has need of it." Like Jesus sending His disciples for the donkey, do you think the lumberyard would give it to you? Of course.

That is what it means to watch and pray with Jesus. We are no longer in the Garden, a stone's throw away from Jesus. **We are now actually seated with *Him* on His throne in the heavenly realms where the business of the universe is transacted.** Like the old gospel preachers were want to say, "if that doesn't spark a fire in your heart for prayer, your wood is wet!"

For further meditation and application:

In the light of this idea of praying *with Jesus*, think of a concern that you have been taking to the Lord in prayer. Are there any ways in which you might change the way you pray?

6

Prayer as a Safeguard Against Evil

But seek the welfare of the city where I have sent you into exile, and pray to the LORD on its behalf, for in its welfare you will find your welfare. Jeremiah 29:7 NIV

Senseless school, marketplace and workplace mass shootings so often monopolizing our news media raise many questions. Not the least of which "could it have been avoided?" As with past massacres such as the 2012 Newtown, Connecticut, school shootings, many things come to the fore that shoulda woulda coulda been done to prevent such tragedies. But I have not heard, at least through secular media, even a hint or suggestion that it could have been avoided through prayer. To even suggest that prayer might have headed off such a tragedy doubtless jars the sensibilities of some, but let us stop for a moment and consider it as a possibility.

In the bible, both Old and New Testaments there are numerous accounts of earnest, concentrated prayer being made where tragedy was thereby averted Jerusalem's last minute deliverance from its own imminent demise when surrounded by the Assyrians during the reign of King Hezekiah was a direct and miraculous answer to prayer. The Apostle Peter's eleventh hour escape from prison and certain death directly coincided with a prayer meeting that was focused on his behalf (2 Kings 19; Acts 12:5-16).

Even more noteworthy is the fact that throughout the Bible God actually encourages individuals to take up positions as watchmen in prayer specifically for the purpose of being a safeguard against evil. Many of the prophets, including Isaiah, Ezekiel, Micah, and Habakkuk were specifically called by God as watchmen to intercede on behalf of God's purposes in the nations. God told Isaiah "I have posted watchmen on your walls, Jerusalem; they will never be silent day or night. You who call on the LORD, give yourselves no rest, and give Him no rest till He establishes Jerusalem and makes her the praise of the earth" (Isaiah 62:6-7 NIV).

Throughout his earthly ministry Jesus encouraged prayer as a preventative against evil. He did so both by example and in His teaching. In His great high priestly prayer in John 17, He prayed for all those the Father had given Him that they might be protected "from the evil one" (vs. 15). When His disciples asked Him how to pray, He urged, "Pray then in this way . . . *deliver us from evil*" (Matthew 6:9; 13 ESV *emphasis added*).

Jesus frequently acknowledged evil as a clear and present danger in the world, and labeled the instigator as the devil and his evil spirits. At one point He declared, "Offenses will certainly come, but woe to the one they come through" (Luke 17:1 KJV). He battled demonic evil on many fronts through prayer and rebuking them with the word, binding and casting them out, and sending His disciples out to do the same.

The intensity of this spiritual warfare came to a focal point as He agonized in prayer the night before He was betrayed in the Garden of Gethsemane. It was there, when He was looking for prayer support and found His disciples sleeping, that He issued what has become the clarion call to watchman intercession. "Could you not watch with me one hour? Watch and pray that you may not enter into temptation. The spirit indeed is willing, but the flesh is weak" (Matthew 26:40-41 ESV).

As we look at this most serious of calls to prayer, there are four arresting features.

First, Jesus is asking for a COMMITMENT TO PRAYER FOR A SET PERIOD OF TIME. In this instance it is specifically an hour, and that period of time is not without significance. An hour carries with it a sense of completeness or accomplishment. When we undertake to do anything for an hour we usually think of that passage of time as long enough to make significant headway.

Second, it is an invitation to TIME SPENT WATCHING "WITH" JESUS. Jesus promises to be *with* us in this venture, to show us what to pray for and how to pray. Much more could be said about this, but suffice it to say that the "watchman ministry" is first and foremost simply watching to see what God is doing and seeking to therefore pray in concert *with* Him.

Third, watching and praying is the primary means instituted by God for GUARDING AGAINST EVIL. At a minimum, those who pray are given a winning advantage over the evil one and his temptation, when they purpose to draw near to God. "Submit yourselves, then, to God. Resist the devil, and he will flee from you. Come near to God and He will come near to you" (James 4:7-8 NIV).

Fourth and finally, undertaking a watchman prayer ministry takes PERSONAL DISCIPLINE. It is not something most people do without a focused decision and concerted effort. Practical steps to incorporate discipline into our prayer lives are presented the next chapter, *Five Steps to Establishing a One Hour Watch.*

Now back to the original question, can tragedies like mass murders be prevented through prayer? Given the preceding overview of the Scriptures on this topic, most definitely! Imagine the potential to alter the spiritual atmosphere in a local community if there were key watchmen intercessors praying daily for God's protection over their public and private institutions. The most immediate concern of any watchman is the city and area where he or she has their residence. This is an established spiritual principle dating back to the Jewish exiles in Babylon when God said, "But seek the welfare of the city where I have sent you into exile, and pray to the LORD on its behalf, for in its welfare you will find your welfare" (Jeremiah 29:7 NIV).

What would happen if God raised up each church to be a light house of prayer that was praying earnestly for the spiritual and natural welfare of their community? What if specific prayers were bombarding heaven to thwart the plans of every schemer of wickedness, mentally deranged, demon possessed, mass murderer, terrorist, arms fanatic and Islamic radical? Just maybe, disaster could be avoided as it was in a 2013, attempted school shooting in Decatur, Georgia. There, a Spirit-empowered Christian working at the front desk, named Antoinette Tuff, headed off another school tragedy by talking a young man toting an AK-47 type weapon into surrendering himself to authorities.

Prayer makes a difference - we know that. How much of a difference, I believe, depends on the intensity and consistency of watchmen intercessors who, like Daniel, Esther, and Moses, are willing to make the commitment to "build up the wall and stand in the gap before" God in prayer no matter what the cost (Ezekiel 22:30 NASB).

There is an appeal by God in the Bible to "seek the welfare of the city where I have sent you into exile, and pray to the LORD on its behalf, for in its welfare you will find your welfare" (Jeremiah 29:7 ESV). **It is sobering to consider, that the difference in our community between security or chaos, life or death, could literally depend upon our prayers.**

For further meditation and application:

With all of this in mind, do you hear the Lord tugging on your heart to "watch with Him one hour" on behalf of your community? What might that look like and what kind of help do you need in beginning to make it happen?

7

Five Steps to Establish an Hour of Prayer

In the morning, O LORD, You will hear my voice.
Psalm 5:3a NASB

There are five very practical things a person can do to help establish a faithful hour of prayer each day. These simple steps of commitment are based upon the Biblical practices of both Old and New Testament saints. Subsequent adherents to these practices in the past two millennia of church history have also proven their indispensable worth in establishing consistent times of prayer.

God takes delight in our initiatives in praying to Him (Proverbs 15:8). **One of the wonders of a prayer commitment is that what begins as a discipline soon becomes our delight as well.** It is the Spirit of God working within us, causing us "both to will and to do His good pleasure" (Philippians 2:13 KJV).

Here, then, are five steps of commitment which we can implement in order to establish a consistent hour of prayer:

1. PRIORITY - Recognize that your time with God is the most important thing you can do each day and make a commitment to do that before all else! David, Jesus, and the disciples, all made an overt commitment to making daily time in prayer their top priority. David vowed "In the morning, O LORD, You will hear my voice; in the morning I will order my prayer to You and eagerly watch" (Psalm 5:3 NASB). Jesus, our quintessential example, incorporated that same prayer priority into His life on a consistent basis. "Before daybreak the next morning, Jesus got up and went out to an isolated place to pray" (Mark 1:35 NLT). Finally, the apostles, who were so deeply impacted by Jesus example, declared their intention to devote themselves to prayer as a first priority, even in the face of growing leadership demands (Acts 6:4).

2. PERIOD OF TIME – Select a specific time for your "hour of prayer," and treat it as the most important appointment you have each day. Think of it the way you would an appointment with your boss, a wealthy benefactor, or a doctor. For simplicity's sake, select a start and ending time. Jesus said "Could you not watch with me one hour?" (Matthew 26:40 ESV). The "one hour" is not meant to be a law, but it is a worthy goal. Start with a length of time you know is doable, like five to ten minutes, and then, as the discipline becomes a delight, the time allotment for it will naturally increase.

Daniel and David were lions when it came to their prayer commitments and can inspire us as we grow in the grace of

prayer. Daniel prayed religiously three times a day, no matter what the circumstances or opposition (Daniel 6:10). It almost cost him his life. David established a routine of praying seven times a day, which included morning, noon, evening, night watches, and before dawn (Psalm 55:17; 119:147-148; 164). As a result, prayer eventually became like breathing for David, and he found himself meditating upon the Lord all day long (Psalm 119:97).

3. PLACE - Choose a place free from interruptions and distractions that enables you to enter into a time of focusing your full attention on God and listening for His voice. Having a regular meeting place for God that readily provides such an atmosphere is absolutely essential for an effective time of prayer! Jesus referred to this place as a "prayer closet" (Matthew 6:6). This is why He repeatedly sought out a solitary place for His own times of prayer (Mark 1:35; Luke 4:42).

4. PERSISTENCE - Fight all delays and interruptions fiercely! Truth be told, it takes a fight of faith to guard the time and the place we set aside for prayer and persistence to keep praying in the face of adversity (1 Timothy 6:12). Jesus encourages us with these words: we "should always pray and never give up" (Luke 18:1 NLT). Paul exhorts "Neither give place to the Devil" (Ephesians 4:27 KJV). In the light of this advice, decide now that you are going to fight to protect your time with God.

5. PLAN OF ACTION - Select a prayer format and Bible study plan that can provide helpful structure in overcoming distraction and indecision and get you

launched into a faith-filled time of prayer. I'll share more on the necessity and benefits of structure in the next chapter. Suffice it to say "those who fail to plan, plan to fail." Sadly, this is all too common when it comes to sustaining a commitment to prayer. Having a plan of action makes the difference between success and failure.

Prayer Formats - An effective prayer format provides two things. It serves as a sequential guide for a pray-er to navigate through important essential elements and topics of prayer, and it helps the pray-er to stay focused.

The following are some commonly used prayer formats:

    a) The Lord's Prayer – Use as a topical outline of prayer (Matthew 6:9-13). See Chapter 14: *Praying the Lord's Prayer*.

    b) John 17 – Jesus' great high priestly prayer. See Chapter 16: *Pray Like Jesus for Family and Friends*.

    c) A-C-T-S Acronym – Adoration, Confession, Thanksgiving, Supplication.

    d) P-R-A-Y Acronym – Praise, Repent, Ask, Yield.

    e) Written Prayer Lists.

    f) Crafted Prayer – See Chapter 12: *Making a Case for Crafted Prayer* and Chapter 13: *Crafted Prayer – Turning Promises into Prayers*.

    g) Use of Written/Memorized Prayers - Prayer Books, Scripture verses, crafted prayer etc.

    h) Liturgy of the Hours or Divine Office – A set of daily prayers (Catholic, Orthodox, Anglican, Lutheran traditions) consisting of hymns, psalms, prayers, and scripture readings.

    i) The Psalms.

j) Lectio Divina - Scripture reading with meditation and prayer. Emerged from Western Monastic Communities: Origen (3rd AD), Desert Fathers (4th AD), Ambrose & Augustine (400 AD), and Benedict (500 AD).

Bible Study Plans – A Bible study plan provides the reader with a roadmap to navigate the Scriptures in a systematic way while making it easy to learn and to store God's Word in the heart. It eliminates the guesswork and ambiguity of having to daily decide what to read and dispenses with a naïve and shallow approach to the Scriptures.

The following are some of the commonly used Bible reading plans:
a) Read it Entirely - over the course of a year or more.
b) Read it by Topical Studies.
c) Read it by Books - over time or in one sitting.
d) Read it by Need.
e) Read it by Chapter.
f) Read from the Psalms or Proverbs regularly.
g) Use Online Bible Reading Plans. Check out websites such as *YouVersion* which provides literally hundreds of different plans and apps for easy use and tracking.
h) Use Bible Study Helps and Online Resources. e.g. *Bible Hub* or *BibleGateway*
i) Write in your Bible. Underline, highlight, and write notes in the margins.
j) Keep a Notebook or Journal – Take time to record the significant things God is saying and doing in your life. It will prove to be of inestimable worth providing

understanding and perspective as to how God is working in and through your life.

For further meditation and application:

In reviewing these five steps of commitment, which one step stands out to you as the most critically helpful thing you can do to help you improve your time of prayer each day? What will it take for you to put this into practice? When will you start?

8

Structure and Spontaneity in Prayer

New wine must be poured into new wineskins.
Luke 5:38 NIV

One of the biggest challenges with regard to prayer is to develop a frequent, extended time of prayer that is at the same time energizing and sustainable over the long haul. Since prayer is the means by which we communicate with God, who is our creator and the lover of our souls, why should it not be so? I am of the strong conviction that, indeed, it can be so and is in fact our rightful inheritance as children of God.

But how is it possible? **The secret lies in utilizing and blending two seemingly incongruous approaches to prayer - structure and spontaneity.** I share this out of my own experiences in the trenches of prayer and the observation of the experience of many others. Most importantly, a strong case can be made from both a Biblical perspective and common historical practice that developing a vibrant and sustainable prayer life depends upon striking a balance between structure and spontaneity.

Before I delve into the practicalities of how to do that let me define the terms I have chosen to describe the kind of prayer life I believe God intends for each of us to have. In the opening sentence I described the ideal prayer life with four words: frequent, extended, energizing and sustainable.

As with every close relationship, there are key elements that contribute to its healthy maintenance. The same principles apply to prayer and our relationship with God. First, communication and interaction must be *frequent*, meaning at a minimum daily, if not often throughout the day. It must also be *extended*, meaning of sufficient time to allow for in-depth and intimate conversation. (It's worth noting that Jesus asked for an hour in the garden.) Third, communication with God is meant to be *energizing*, meaning that it should be a life-giving, joyful experience that is nurturing, enriching and inspiring. And finally a healthy prayer life needs to be *sustainable*. In other words it *continues* to develop and deepen over the long haul, through thick and thin, trial and triumph.

Now what do I mean by structure and spontaneity? The two obviously are opposites but, like the wineskin and the wine, it takes both to have a party! By structure I am referring to a disciplined commitment to the repeated use of set times and prescribed ways of praying. Such commitments provide initiative and motivation to overcome prayer-less inertia. Structure is like a launch pad or rocket launcher that is necessary to initiate and propel our prayers into their intended trajectory to the heavenly realms where they accomplish God's purposes. Structure enables us to overcome distractions and diversions by guiding and giving focus to our prayers. Furthermore, as with any discipline, structure empowers us to break through the "spirit is willing, but the flesh is weak" syndrome (Matthew 26:41).

Practically speaking, structure in prayer is applied in one or more of the following ways:

1. Regular use of a predetermined scheduled prayer time. David praised God seven times a day, Daniel prayed three times a day (Psalm 119:164; Daniel 6:10).

2. Regularly attending and praying with a selected group of fellow pray-ers. Believers continually devoted themselves to "the breaking of bread and to prayer" and the apostles observed the hours of prayer established at the Temple (Acts 2:42; 3:1).

3. Regular use of a set place and/or posture for prayer. Jesus consistently sought out a solitary place for prayer, be it on a mountain, in the garden.

4. Regular use of a prescribed or chosen topical list, format, outline and/or formal liturgy for prayer. E.g. The Lord's Prayer, ACTS (Adoration, Confession, Thanksgiving, Supplication) or the Liturgy of the Hours.

5. Regular use of written or memorized scriptures and crafted prayers (see Chapters 12 and 13).

Whereas structure provides a framework or launching pad for prayer, spontaneity provides the fuel empowering our

prayers and the guidance system helping our prayers to find their mark.

Spontaneity in prayer is best defined as the freedom and flexibility to respond to the leading of the Holy Spirit. Attentiveness to the spontaneity of the Spirit is absolutely necessary in prayer because it is through the Holy Spirit that revelation, faith, and God's power are all released (Zechariah 4:6). It is the Spirit that "helps us in our weakness," teaches how to pray, and, when necessary, even intercedes for us (Romans 8:26).

The necessity of a blend of structure and spontaneity in spiritual matters is seen throughout the scripture, beginning with the inherent marriage of Word and Spirit. Structure is like the Word or Bible (Greek - *logos*), and spontaneity is like the Spirit-inspired word (Greek - *rhema*). We are told that although the law (structure) came through Moses, Jesus came to fulfill the law as the embodiment of both truth (structure) and grace (spontaneity) (John 1:17).

Church history is replete with Christian traditions that nurtured frequent, extended, energizing and sustainable prayer through a blend of both structure and the spontaneity of the Holy Spirit. Just to mention a few, there were the Desert Fathers, St. Patrick and the Celts, St. Benedict, Count Zinzendorf and the Moravians, William Booth and the Salvation Army, and the Azusa Street Revival. All of these Christian movements, although placing a varying emphasis on either structure or spontaneity, maintained a blend of both, and thereby sustained years of history-shaping prayer.

As we think about utilizing both structure and spontaneity in our personal prayer lives, it is helpful to think of them like the new wineskins and new wine that Jesus insisted upon in His teaching about the kingdom life. For your prayer life to be vibrant it needs *both* **new wineskin structures** and **new wine spontaneous responses** to the Holy Spirit. Creativity and variety are the keys to keeping and making things new. The use of new prayer structures primes the pump for the Spirit's release of new revelation and faith in prayer.

May I encourage you to experiment with the five types of prayer structures listed above as a launching pad for new spontaneity and accompanying joy to be released in your prayer life?

For further meditation and application:

Think about your times with God in terms of structure and spontaneity. Which one of the two might be a growing edge for you and something you feel you should emphasize more in order to grow your prayer life?

9

Five Secrets to a Consistent, Energized Prayer Life

In the morning I will order my prayer to You and eagerly watch. Psalm 5:3b NASB

David, the shepherd, psalmist and king of the Old Testament, is the author of this remarkable declaration. In it he reveals the secret to a consistent, energized prayer life. The secret is contained in his use of the word "order" to describe the manner in which he prays. There is something compelling about the way David ordered or arranged, his prayer time that drew him back again and again with genuine expectancy. That, coupled with his enjoyment of God's presence, led him to make a commitment to daily take his place before God to watch and pray.

So what is it about his choice of the word "order," to describe his prayer, that led to such an eager commitment to daily watch and pray? The Hebrew word for order, *arak,* means "to arrange" or "set in order." In other places in scripture it is used to describe how they built an altar, arranged wood to light a fire and/or arranged the offering on the altar. It is also used to describe the way in which the showbread was to be arranged and presented to God in the Holy Place (Exodus 40:4). It is used, in reference to the orderly presentation of a legal case (Job 13:18).

Order is one of the first principles instituted by God at creation. It is a means by which God initiates and establishes His purposes in the earth. Most notably we see it in His creation of day and night, seed time and harvest, and through the Sinai covenant, His institution of the tabernacle, system of sacrifices and prescribed approach of the High Priest into the Holy of Holies.

Given the thoughtful and logical way in which God orders things, what then does it mean to order one's prayer life? I believe the ordering of David's prayer had to do with his choice of key elements of prayer and an intentional arrangement of their sequence to bring him into the presence of God. From a study of his life, we can identify at least five things that David did when he prayed that illustrate this intentional arrangement of his prayer time to insure its vibrancy.

1. Praise and Thanksgiving – In the reading of the Psalms we notice immediately that typically the first order of business in David's approach to God was to begin with worship. This priority was reflected in how he instituted singers and musicians to thank and praise God day and night within the tabernacle he erected to house the ark during the years before the temple was built (1 Chronicles 16:4).

It is my conviction, both from Scripture and personal practice, that establishing a vital and vibrant prayer time is directly linked to beginning with praise and thanksgiving. It literally is the doorway that ushers us into the presence of God. That is why we are clearly told "Enter his gates with thanksgiving and his courts with praise; give thanks to him and praise his name" (Psalm 100:4 NIV).

2.   Acknowledgement of Dependence - A critical touch point for David in his prayers to God was always an acknowledgement of his dependence upon God both for the forgiveness of his sins and the carrying of his burdens. He knew that if he tolerated unconfessed iniquity in his heart the Lord would not hear him, and so he prayed repeatedly for God to cover his transgression and cleanse him from his sin (Psalm 66:18; 51:1-2). The other thing he did without hesitation was to make sure he regularly gave his burdens to God. "Cast your burden on the LORD, and he will sustain you; he will never permit the righteous to be moved" (Psalm 55:22 ESV).

In order to experience an unfettered and rejuvenating time of prayer it is imperative that we make a point of laying all of our sins and burdens at the foot of the cross of Jesus. That secures a freedom from distraction and instills a confidence to proceed in prayer as the Holy Spirit leads.

3.   Confession of God's Promises – The basis of our authority in prayer is the word of God. When we pray God's promises back to Him and declare the beauty of His character as revealed in the Scriptures we align ourselves with His will. He has promised that "if we ask anything according to His will, He hears us. And if we know that He hears us—whatever we ask—we know that we have what we asked of Him" (1 John 5:14-15 NIV).

There is power in praying God's promises that far eclipses praying our problems. Prayers that get answers and energize the pray-ers are prayers that declare the scriptures because faith comes by hearing the word of God proceeding from our own mouths (Romans 10:17). David repeatedly rehearsed God's promises as he prayed, choosing to stand on a foundation of the authority God's word and the faithfulness of His character (Psalm 86:15; 2 Samuel 7:21-29).

4. Responsiveness to the Leading of the Holy Spirit – An ordered or structured approach to prayer is like a launching pad for inspired spontaneity. (See Chapter 8: *Structure and Spontaneity in Prayer*.) Beginning with worship, proceeding through an acknowledgement of dependence upon God, and then moving into a bold profession of God's will in His word positions the pray-er to sense the leading of the Holy Spirit and respond accordingly. In many of David's psalms as he proceeds to pour out his heart, we notice a sudden shift in the tenor and spirit of his prayer. Often he concludes his psalms with confessions of faith and confidence in God (Psalms 6, 7, 11, 13, 16 & 17, just to mention a few). In some we see an ebb and flow throughout the psalm of Spirit-inspired prayer mixed in with the other elements (Psalm 18).

5. Variety – One of the salient features of David's prayers, as demonstrated primarily in the Psalms, is the variety of types and focuses of prayer. There are psalms that are petitions, complaints, laments, spiritual warfare, prophetic declarations, litanies of God's faithfulness, and hymns of praise. There are psalms focused on Israel, the nations, the enemy, the oppressed, the overcomer, the sinner, the forgiven, the past, the future, the wonder of creation, and the glory of God. Variety is the byword, and it is a critical ingredient without which sustainable and energized prayer would not be possible. Paul said it best. "And pray in the Spirit on all occasions with all kinds of prayers and requests" (Ephesians 6:18 NIV).

This list of five ingredients that David used in ordering his prayer is by no means exhaustive. Yet, in the whole scheme of things, I am of the deepest conviction that, when all five are incorporated into a person's daily prayer time, they, like David, will have a sustainable, consistent, energized prayer life. I can personally testify that, by God's grace, my commitment over the years to ordering my daily prayer time using these five keys has reenergized my prayer life and relationship with Him.

For further meditation and application:

As you think about your prayer times in terms of the way in which David ordered his prayers, what similarities and dissimilarities do you find? If you were to pick one ingredient that might energize your prayer life what would it be?

10

Giving Physical Expression to Prayer

I appeal to you therefore, brothers, by the mercies of God, to present your bodies as a living sacrifice, holy and acceptable to God, which is your spiritual worship.
Romans 12:1 ESV

Probably the most common struggle that people have in attempting a focused, sustained, and meaningful prayer time is dealing with distractions associated with a wandering mind. Throughout the ages, one of the great secrets for engaging in effective prayer has been connected to the position a person chooses to assume while praying. By position I mean the posture or attitude our body takes while we communicate our innermost thoughts, through prayer, to God.

While we commune with God from our spirit through both words and sighs too deep for words, there is also an important role our bodies can and should play in expressing our prayers. In a very real sense this is a tangible expression of loving the Lord our God through prayer with all our heart, soul, mind, and strength (body) (Luke 10:27).

The more that prayer expresses the entirety of who we are, spirit, soul *and body*, the more focused and engaged we will become - and in the end the more meaningful our prayer times will be. We can literally present our "bodies as a living sacrifice" when we use them in taking appropriate prayer positions to express outwardly to Him what is in our hearts. In this way we offer our body, His temple, as a holy habitation of spiritual worship for His glory and praise (Romans 12:1).

Practically, what are these prayer positions? Throughout the scriptures both in the Old and New Testaments we see prayer combined with a variety of postures. We find people praying while standing, sitting, kneeling, bowing low, laying prostrate, and even walking. We also see people in these various positions having their heads and eyes lifted toward heaven or bowed with eyes cast down to the ground. In many instances we see that those praying have their hands lifted up and extended to the heavens.

Whatever the posture taken or positions of the hands or head, the one thing we notice is that it becomes a natural expression and extension of the attitude of heart with which we are seeking to communicate with God. While we know the most important thing to God is what is in a person's heart, it is nonetheless notable that He and the writers of the scripture also recorded the attitude expressed in prayer by the pray-ers' bodies.

In my personal prayer life I have found great benefit in using different types of prayer coupled with the use of multiple prayer postures. There are two main reasons for intentionally making it a priority to incorporate the whole spectrum of positions into my prayers. First, as I have studied the great prayers and pray-ers in the Bible it is clear that standing, kneeling, bowing, hands raised etc. were inextricably tied to effective, anointed prayer. Second, I could not help but surmise, since most of my praying has been from a sitting position, that to be more Biblical in my praying I should get off my duff and be more demonstrative in expressing my prayer with action.

What I have discovered has revolutionized my prayer life. The immediate benefits which I have noticed is that praying in this way has helped me focus and put aside distractions as never before. Even better, it has released new levels of faith and confidence that I am genuinely connecting with God.

How has your prayer life been expressed with regard to the use of different postures as you pray? In the next chapter we will look at seven unique ways that a person can use their body in expressing their prayers.

For further meditation and application:

Has your position or posture been an important factor in helping you adequately express and focus your prayers? Are you desirous and/or willing to experiment in using a greater variety of prayer postures to accompany your prayers? Why or why not?

11

Exploring Different Prayer Postures

Love the Lord your God with all your heart and with all your soul and with all your mind and with all your strength. Mark 12:30 NIV

In the last chapter I share several compelling reasons for actively engaging our bodies as we pray. While such actions as kneeling, bowing and lifting hands are commonly recognized as expressive forms of prayer, many people do not incorporate them into their daily practice of prayer. But those who are intentional about loving God in prayer with all their heart, soul, mind, and strength (body) would do well to consider using a variety of prayer postures.

The following is a summary of the seven main ways recorded in the Bible that people, including Jesus, prayed. Hopefully it will stir a hunger in you to give them a try.

1. Kneeling – This position expresses a reverence for God and seriousness of intent by the person praying. It is probably one of the most common ways people prayed and a key posture that can be used in focusing our petitions. Solomon knelt for a long period of time with arms outstretched as he prayed his great prayer dedicating the temple. When he finished, fire fell from heaven (2 Chronicles 6:13). Daniel knelt and prayed three times a day, and we know the amazing results he experienced (Daniel 6:10).

2. Bowing Low – This position expresses fervency and persistence in prayer. One of the best examples is Elijah when he was praying for rain on Mount Carmel. There he prayed seven times while "bowed low to the ground and praying with his face between his knees" (1 Kings 18:42 NLT). We are told he was heard because of his earnest fervency (James 5:17). In the gospels it is common to see people bowing low as they approached Jesus. It was an integral expression of the fervent requests they were bringing to Him.

3. Laying Prostrate – We see in scripture that when people took this position they were typically expressing their humility, utter desperateness and dependency upon God. Moses did it in intercession for Israel (Deuteronomy 9:18). Jesus did it in the Garden of Gethsemane where we are told "He fell with His face to the ground and prayed" (Matthew 26:39 NIV).

As a side note, this particular praying position is even viable when a person is in bed. "When I think of you in bed, I will meditate on you in the night watches" (Psalm 63:6 ISV). So there you go. Whether you are tossing and turning or simply taking your leisure, you can pray effectively even while lying in bed.

4. Standing – This stance is frequently used in conjunction with more aggressive forms of prayer such as spiritual warfare. It expresses the strength of our conviction and the firmness of our insistence on God's triumph over the enemy. Paul urges all of us, in the context of the call to war against principalities and powers and putting on the full armor of God, "to stand firm" for the purpose of prayer (Ephesian 6:13-14).

5. Walking – The beauty of this posture for prayer is its link to the idea of walking and communing with God. This was His original intention for His creation dating all the way back to the Garden of Eden. Adam walked with God, communing with Him in the cool of the day. Enoch walked with God, and their communion was so sweet that, at the end of one walk, God decided to take Enoch home with Him (Genesis 5:24). Prayer walks are great for dialoguing with God, especially when walking in nature.

6. Sitting – This posture is often associated with listening in stillness for God and enjoying His presence, as with contemplative and centering prayer. A picture I love is that of King David going into the tabernacle and simply sitting in God's presence before the ark of the covenant (2 Samuel 7:18).

7. Raising Hands and Eyes to Heaven – This posture expresses adoration, surrender, and yielded dependence upon God in childlike faith and expectation. Numerous times the psalmists urge the worshipers of God to lift up their hands. In the New Testament, Paul makes the same appeal: "I desire then that in every place the men should pray, lifting holy hands without anger or quarreling" (1

Timothy 2:8 ESV). Jesus, in His praying, often lifted His eyes to His Father in heaven. He knew, as should we, that our help comes only from one place, and that is from above (John 11:14; 17:1; James 1:17).

I hope that your appetite has been whetted to give these different positions for prayer an earnest try. Why not experiment with them? If you are struggling with distractions and staying focused while you pray, these should help.

For further meditation and application:

Pick one of these prayer postures that you seldom use and incorporate it into your times of prayer over the next week. Make a note of the effect it has upon your praying and adjust your approach to prayer accordingly.

12

Making a Case for Crafted Prayer

The prayer recorded is the prayer rewarded!

That is a phrase the Lord spoke to me many years ago, and I have used it to inscribe the inside front cover of each new prayer journal which I begin. **It has been a motivational reminder to me of the power of sealing my prayers in pen and ink so that I can pray them again and again until they are answered.**

It is not a novel idea with me. **The Bible itself is a prayer journal,** with many prayers penned by the likes of Abraham, Moses, David, Solomon, Nehemiah, and the prophets Daniel, Isaiah and Jeremiah. Jesus' unparalleled prayers for His followers are recorded as well, along with the many apostolic prayers throughout the New Testament, not the least of which are Paul's. **Each of these prayers have been prayed over and over again for centuries because they carry the inspiration and anointing of the Holy Spirit while embodying the eternal nature and purposes of God.**

Since the first century, believers in each generation have also recorded their inspired prayers. Many iconic prayers from famous saints and prayer books compiled by various sects exist today as a result. Along with the Biblical models of prayer, these anointed prayers serve us like familiar old friends. They guide us in prayer when we lack for words, or feel like we are groping in the darkness for direction as to how to pray.

Praying these prayers with a humble heart can revive the soul and lend fervency and focus to our prayer life. Since they were obviously penned under the inspiration of the Holy Spirit, they also release faith because we know that they express the will of God. That is what the Apostle John is referring to when he writes, "This is the confidence we have in approaching God: that if we ask anything according to his will, he hears us. And if we know that he hears us--whatever we ask--we know that we have what we asked of him" (1 John 5:14-15 NIV).

Understanding this basic prayer principle and applying it in our everyday communication with God will vitalize our prayer lives. Not only that, praying scriptures and other God-breathed prayers introduces an eternal quality to our praying that transcends time and space. Such prayer carries a cumulative effect as it is coupled with similar prayers prayed by yourself and others all the way from the past to the present.

And here is an even more provocative thought. Why not record your own inspired, Holy Spirit anointed prayers? In so doing, you can pray them again and again, while each time rekindling the same passion and faith you had when you first were energized to pray them. Since, in most cases, they may have been given at a point of focused need, these prayers are like a precious revelation given by God to aid you in contending for their fulfillment.

This form of prayer can be generated in several ways. **One familiar form is termed crafted prayer.** Crafted prayer is a deliberate engagement with the Lord through worship, Bible reading, and meditation upon appropriate scriptures with the goal in mind of writing out a prayer that expresses the cry of your heart for what you desire. What has been written can then be prayed repeatedly and even shared with others, asking them to agree in prayer with you.

Another form of recorded prayer, one I have found to be even more personally powerful, is what I would call revelatory prayer. These are prayers that are given spontaneously by the Holy Spirit in the heat of battle, so to speak. They are words or phrases that a person in the midst of a time of fervent prayer can find themselves speaking out, declaring and often repeating. They may be quotations of scripture promises and/or simply godly thoughts. Regardless, they seem to carry an authority in the Spirit with an insistent determination and belief that they are God-breathed. They are words that carry an anointing with creative power to literally produce or arrange their desired end.

Capturing such prayers for the purpose of repeating them as we contend for their answers is doubtless an imperative. When God speaks into our lives by revelation, it is incumbent upon us to record it. For me, keeping a prayer journal has been a great aid in doing just that. I would have to say that the prayer recorded *has* been rewarded as I have prayed it again and again.

Lately, the Lord has helped me take this form of revelatory praying to a new level. My most effective praying is seldom accomplished while sitting with pen and journal in hand. I much prefer walking, kneeling, or lying prostrate on the floor. It is in those moments of animated prayer that the release of revelation is most likely to happen. When the Holy Spirit begins to give me anointed words or phrases, I am not always able to pause and write them down.

I have discovered that, by using a little hand held digital recorder, I can now record my prayers as I am speaking them. Later, when I am done praying, at my convenience, I can transcribe them into my journal. That way I am able to revisit those anointed prayers with their God-breathed wording again and again, each time recapturing the fervency and faith which accompanied them the first time I prayed them.

Let me challenge you, if you are not taking advantage of this amazing form of prayer, it's time for you to consider doing so. Our relationship with God through prayer is of paramount importance. Why should you neglect to use every tool available in your prayer arsenal? Not the least of which is "the prayer recorded is the prayer rewarded." In the next chapter we will explore some practical how tos in writing crafted prayers.

For further meditation and application:

What for you is the most compelling reason to use crafted prayer as an important ingredient of your prayer life? If you have never written a crafted prayer, are you willing to give it a try? Why or why not?

13

Crafted Prayer -
Turning Promises into Prayers

If you keep knocking long enough, he will get up and give you whatever you need because of your shameless persistence. Luke 11:8 NLT

One of the virtues of prayer that Jesus specifically encouraged was that of persistence. He gave illustrations to drive this important truth home by telling parables about such people as the audacious friend needing bread at midnight and the persistent widow badgering the unjust judge (Luke 11:5-9; Luke 18:1-5).

While initially God's silence or seeming lack of response to our prayers may appear to be a "no," it typically is more like a "not yet." Timing, as they say, is everything. There is with God a mystery in His ways that requires an attitude of dependently waiting upon Him for the answer. The preparation process in delivering an answer is as much, if not more, about what He is doing *in* us as it is about what He plans on doing *for* us.

The one practice which I have found to be the most helpful in praying persistent prayers over the long haul is that of turning His promises into prayers. Here are some practical tips, by no means original with me, for doing that.

1.)   Each day as I am reading the Bible, I seek to be sensitive to the Holy Spirit to speak to me a "word of life" (John 6:63). It is an encouraging verse or passage of scripture that speaks specifically to a need or situation I am facing.

2.)   When that happens, I seek to "capture" that truth as a promise from God just for me. I highlight it in my Bible and write a date, sometimes with a brief comment, beside it.

3.) Next, I copy the passage into my prayer journal and also write about its significance in my life and what I believe God is saying to me through it.

4.) Then, and this is the critical part, I take that scripture and personalize it by crafting a prayer. That means writing out a prayer that can be prayed in the first person with that passage of scripture as the basis.

5) Finally, I commit to praying that crafted prayer on a regular basis. Along with other such prayers that I have written, it has become a daily touch point in my relationship with God.

The power in praying God's promises is that we are using *His* own words, imbued with *His* anointing. Praying the promises of God is as old as His Word. When we pray this way we are emulating the men and women of the Bible who sought His favor by reminding Him of what He had said and promised.

Like the shamelessly persistent man in the Luke 11 parable of Jesus I have found that my regular knocking on heaven's door eventually gets the same results. And in the mean time I have been sustained and enriched by God's promises for me.

Why not give crafted prayer a try? It promises to enrich your prayer life and also help you in praying persistent faith-filled prayers.

Here is an example of a portion of a crafted prayer I wrote for the salvation of a friend using Ephesians 1:17-19, John 14:6, and Matthew 11:27:

I keep asking glorious Father, God of our Lord Jesus Christ, that you will give _____ the Spirit of wisdom and revelation, so that he/she may know you. I pray that the eyes of his/her heart may be enlightened in order that he/she may know the hope to which you have called him/her, the riches of your glorious inheritance in the saints, and your incomparably great power for us who believe (Ephesians 1:17-19). Jesus you said "I am the way and the truth and the life, no one comes to Father except through me." "No one knows the Father except the son and anyone the son chooses to reveal him" (John 14:6; Matthew 11:27). Therefore Jesus, according to your Word would you please reveal the Father to _____?

For further meditation and application:

Can you identify a concern or burden that you have been carrying for some time in prayer? Are there some scripture promises that you have been holding onto and standing upon as you pray? If so, you have the beginnings of a crafted prayer. Write a short prayer personalizing one of those scriptures by changing the wording to include the person or thing you are praying about. Then commit to reading/praying that scripture prayer whenever you lift up that burden to the Lord.

14

Praying the Lord's Prayer

Lord, teach us to pray. Luke 11:1 NIV

What has come to be called the "Lord's Prayer" was originally a teaching on prayer that Jesus gave to His disciples. They were so impressed and impacted by the manner in which He prayed that one day they asked Him, "Lord, teach us to pray" (Luke 11:1 NIV). Jesus responded by directing His disciples into their own relationship with the Father through prayer. He outlined for them the essential elements, or touch points, the Father heart of God invites all of His creation to bring to Him. The pattern He provided also gave indication that the sequence in which these things were addressed had significance.

The Lord's Prayer therefore, is much more than a short, succinct prayer to be recited. It is a pathway into the heart of the Father. When it is approached as a topical outline for prayer it reveals to us the "depths of the riches of the wisdom and the knowledge of God" (Romans 11:33 NIV).

Therefore, what follows, given phrase by phrase, topic by topic, in the sequence Jesus prescribed, is the most all-encompassing prayer ever crafted. For simplicity's sake and for ease in applying these critical prayer points, I am providing a focus for each and using phrasing in the outline that addresses you, the reader, as it relates to your prayer life.

1. PRAISE - Focus: God's Glory
"Our Father which art in heaven, hallowed be Thy name" (Matthew 6:9 KJV).

Throughout the Scriptures, we see praise as the starting point for any time of prayer. The Father is worthy of praise and glory simply for who He is. Begin by focusing your attention on God and His Character. Reflect on His loving nature and faithfulness to you and others over the past few days. Offer praise and specific thanksgiving for what He has done. Ask that His Name be glorified in the earth through you and other Christians.

2. PURPOSES - Focus: Furtherance of His Kingdom on Earth
"Thy kingdom come" (Matthew 6:10a KJV).

Pray for the extension of the kingdom of God both locally and globally through the furtherance of the Gospel and salvation in Jesus' name. Ask God to give you a global perspective for what He is doing in the nations. Pray that the church might become a House of Prayer for all Nations.

3. PRIORITIES - Focus: His Rule in Your Life & Your World
"Thy will be done on earth as it is in heaven" (Matthew 6:10b KJV).

Pray for the increase of the rule and reign of King Jesus, beginning in your own life and extending to all those around you. Surrender afresh your will, your plans, and your life to the Lordship of Jesus. Ask God to fill you afresh with His Holy Spirit, and yield to His control. Pray for God's will for your loved ones, church, workplace, city, state, nation, and the world.

4. PROVISION - Focus: His Provision
"Give us this day our daily bread" (Matthew 6:11 KJV).
Acknowledge your dependency upon God to meet every need in your life. Pray specifically for God to meet those needs both for you and for others. Examine your motives, being sure that what you are asking for will please God.

5. PARDON & RELATIONSHIPS - Focus: Forgiveness
"And forgive us our debts as we forgive our debtors" (Matthew 6:12 KJV).
Ask God to search your heart for any unconfessed sin. Confess those sins to Him and receive His forgiveness. Make a specific point to forgive and release anyone who may have offended you.

6. PRECAUTIONS - Focus: Guidance
"And lead us not into temptation (testing)" (Matthew 6:13a KJV).
Ask God to guide you in your decisions regarding where you go, what you do, and how you spend your time. Ask God to keep you spiritually alert to ways in which your flesh and the devil may test you or try to hinder you or your loved ones from doing God's will.

7. PROTECTION - Focus: Protection from Evil
"But deliver us from evil" (Matthew 6:13b KJV).

Ask for God's protection over yourself, your loved ones, the church, and the nation. Take the authority given you as a child of God, and command every evil power seeking to influence your life to be bound in the mighty name of Jesus Christ.

8. PRAISE & THANKSGIVING - Focus: Thanksgiving
"For Thine is the kingdom and the power and the glory forever" (Matthew 6:13c KJV).

Always conclude your prayer with praise and thanksgiving. It is a declaration in faith that God has heard your requests and the answers are already on the way (1 John 5:15).

For further meditation and application:

Set aside a day soon to spend time with God, using this outline of the Lord's Prayer. Then pause to evaluate how it could improve your prayer relationship with the Father.

15

The Why and How of Prayer Mandates

As for me, far be it from me that I should sin against the LORD by failing to pray for you. 1 Samuel 12:23 NIV

The prophet Samuel, in his farewell address and final warnings to Israel, reminds them of his faithfulness to fulfill God's mandate upon his life to pray for them. My use of the word mandate to describe his prayer commitment is intentional because it refers to a royal command or authorization to act in a particular way. In this instance, Samuel's prayer mandate from the Lord is so serious that he would consider it a sin if he did not do it.

A prayer mandate is a sacred trust in which God conscripts His prayer watchmen and warriors to intercede on behalf of particular groups of people for the fulfillment of His purposes in their lives.

Prayer mandates are common throughout the Bible. They reveal God's heart and intentions for His creation. They are invitations to enter into the implementation of God's sovereign plans in the earth. Prayer mandates gripped the lives of Abraham, Moses, Isaiah, Jeremiah, Daniel, and Esther, just to mention a few of the Old Testament saints.

In the New Testament, the apostle Paul repeatedly makes reference to his unceasing, night-and-day prayer for the churches that he established (Colossians 1:9; 1 Thessalonians 3:10; 2 Timothy 1:3 etc.). At one point in reference to this mandate he confesses, "I face daily the pressure of my concern for all the churches" (2 Corinthians 11:28 NIV).

It is not unusual to receive multiple prayer mandates from God. Paul reveals that he also had a mandate from God to pray for Israel's salvation. "Brothers and sisters, my heart's desire and prayer to God for the Israelites is that they may be saved" (Romans 10:1 NIV).

One of the best examples of a prayer mandate in action is the prayer that Jesus prays in John 17. In His prayer, He clearly delineates His mandate when He says He is praying to the Father for a very specific group of people: "for all those you have given me" (vs. 2; 6) and for "those who will believe in me through their message" (vs. 20). "I pray for them. I am not praying for the world but for those you have given me, for they are yours" (John 17:9 NIV). In the next chapter I'll share some practical ways to use John 17 to pray for those whom God has given us as a mandate for prayer.

Prayer mandates provide a rhythm to our life of prayer by assigning us a priority to pray regularly for particular groups of people. Such mandates give us specific focus and direction for prayer that, when revisited again and again, add a depth of increasing revelation, wisdom, and authority.

My prayer life has been enriched immeasurably by giving attention to the prayer mandates that God has set before me. By way of personal testimony, I pray that if you have struggled in establishing a rhythm of prayer you may be encouraged by what I am learning. As I have sought the Lord for clarity on my prayer mandates, I have identified seven distinct groups of people for whom I am specifically responsible to pray.

For simplicities sake I have assigned a specific mandate to each day of the week: Mondays – My City and County; Tuesdays - The Persecuted and Suffering of the World; Wednesdays – The Nations (Specific nations as the Holy Spirit leads); Thursdays – My State and the United States; Fridays – Israel; Saturdays – Family & Friends; and Sundays – The Church. In my regular rhythm of praying weekly for each mandate, I have added appropriate scripture promises and professions while developing an ever changing list of specific people and things for which to pray.

Now by force of habit, each morning when I awake my mind and spirit immediately gravitate to prayer for the mandate of the day. By use of my accumulated revelation and knowledge on the topic, crafted prayer, and sensitivity to the Holy Spirit, I now find it is easy to launch into sustainable and energized prayer. Another thing that I am noticing is the burden for the mandate is carrying beyond my morning prayer time into my consciousness as prayer reminders throughout the day.

One other thing that has helped with each mandate is taking advantage of resources available to keep me updated on current developments. Subscriptions on selected topics to news services like *Google Alerts* is an easy way to stay informed and pray both in the Spirit and with the understanding (1 Corinthians 14:15).

It is my conviction that both individuals and churches would do well to seek God to identify their respective prayer mandates. They provide an energizing, unifying factor in prayer that most importantly is a sharing in the heart and purposes of God for His world. Oh, that we might continually press on to know the Lord!

For further meditation and application:

Which group(s) of people has God given you responsibility to pray for? Do you have one or more prayer mandates that God has given you as a sacred trust of intercession? If you are not sure, ask the Holy Spirit to help you discern where you carry a passionate concern about someone or something. Those "concerns" might just be your mandate(s).

16

Pray Like Jesus for Family and Friends

I pray for them. I am not praying for the world but for those you have given me, for they are yours. John 17:9 NIV

Have you ever struggled to pray regularly for the people God has placed in your life? I know I have. Like many people, for years I used a prayer list of all my family and friends as a helpful place to begin. But even then I often had difficulty staying focused and praying meaningful, confident prayers for many of them. Invariably I would gravitate merely to a rote recitation of their names as I moved down the list.

It was not, however, until I discovered a Biblical, tried and true *way* to effectively pray for them that a new focus and faith began to energize my prayers.

There is one chapter in the Bible that is dedicated entirely to a verbatim prayer recited by Jesus. That chapter is John 17, and it is considered to be one of the great treasures in all of scripture because it preserves for posterity an entire prayer, prayed by the greatest pray-er who ever lived! Some have called it Jesus' great High Priestly Prayer. As stated in the last chapter, it is also one of the best examples there is of a prayer mandate because Jesus is praying for those the Father had committed to His care.

Apart from the first verse which says "After Jesus said this, he looked toward heaven and prayed," everything that follows is in red letters. They are the words of Jesus as He prays to the Father for a very specific group of people: "for all those you have given me" (vs. 2; 6) and for "those who will believe in me through their message" (vs. 20). In fact, Jesus specifically narrows the field by saying, "I am *not* praying for the world, *but* for those you have given me."

Who then is this select group for whom Jesus was praying? They were His apostles and disciples. Interestingly this included dear friends such as Lazarus, Mary and Martha, Mary Magdalene, and family such as His mother, brothers, and cousins.

The John 17 prayer of Jesus is therefore the best model ever given for our use in praying for those whom God has placed in our lives. A study of the prayer reveals that there are seven specific ways in which Jesus prayed for His loved ones.

These seven prayers lend a Biblical specificity to our prayers and inspire confidence and faith as we pray because we are praying the same words Jesus prayed. Praying

Scripture has always been a sure-fire way to pray effectively, and to me this way of praying for friends and family is as exciting and powerful as it gets. This is so because "this is the confidence we have in approaching God: that if we ask anything according to his will, he hears us" (1 John 5:14 NIV).

Here are seven prayers you can use to pray following in Jesus' footsteps: "Father...

1. GLORIFY Jesus through their lives by having them do the work you've given them to do. – "Glorify your Son that the Son may glorify you" (vs. 1b). "I brought you glory on earth by finishing the work you gave me to do" (vs. 4).

2. FORTIFY and protect them from the evil one and keep them safe in Jesus name. – "Protect them from the evil one" (vs. 15).

3. UNIFY them and make them one with you and with one another. – "...that all of them may be one" (vs. 21).

4. SANCTIFY them in the truth of your Word. – Set them apart for you, and make them holy. "Sanctify them by the truth; your word is truth." (vs. 17)

5. MULTIPLY them by sending them into the world with your message. - "I have sent them into the world . . . so that the world may believe" (vs. 18; 21).

6. FILL them with your Joy. – "...so that they may have the full measure of my joy within them" (vs. 13).

7. REVEAL your Presence and Glory to them. – "Father, I want those you have given me to be with me where I am, and to see my glory" (vs. 24).

As you consider all the precious people God has placed in your life, why not pray the prayer Jesus prayed for them?

For further meditation and application:

The next time you pray through your prayer list of family, relatives, and friends, consider using these seven prayers from John 17. As you pray for each person, pause and select the appropriate prayer(s) that is applicable to their situation and your burden for them. Pray for them using the same words and phrases that Jesus used in praying for those the Father had given him. Expect a quickening of your faith, and renewed confidence as you pray, that God is hearing and answering your prayers.

17

Make Me a House of Prayer

And Jesus began to teach and say to them, "Is it not written, 'My house shall be called a house of prayer for all nations?'"
Mark 11:17 NIV

The context in which Jesus said this was during His historic cleansing of the temple in Jerusalem. It took place the very week leading up to His eventual betrayal and crucifixion. He had just driven out all the merchants and money changers. The teeming crowds gathered there in preparation for Passover were doubtless standing in stunned silence, astonished at the demonstrative way in which the great, revered teacher had underscored His point. He made two extraordinary statements. First He declared that the Temple was His house, a claim which, if made by any other person, would be blasphemy. Second, He insisted that His house's salient, defining purpose was to be a house of prayer.

Several days later, on that agonizing night in the Garden of Gethsemane, He issued a similar call to prayer to His own disciples. "Could you not watch with me one hour?

Keep watch and pray, so that you will not give in to temptation. For the spirit is willing, but the flesh is weak" (Mark 14:38 NIV).

The problem of prayerlessness, both in corporate worship settings and in the private devotional lives of individuals, is very much with us yet today. In fact, I would venture to say that the most glaring omission, if not the greatest weakness in a majority of church services across this nation on any given Sunday, is the time and commitment given to prayer. By and large, more time is given to every other aspect of the service, including the announcements, than to prayer. Yes, I know that many churches and pastors pray over the offering and before and after the message. But in terms of concerted, sustained, corporate prayer for both personal and public needs, and for local, national, and international concerns, little if any time is allotted.

Why is that? Has religious activity in God's house, and even non-spiritual activity dressed up to look religious, become a substitute for watching and praying? Is it still the case that "the spirit is willing, but the flesh is weak?" Having been a first-hand observer as a worshiper, service planner and leader, and pastor/teacher for over 40 years, I say unequivocally that the answer to all of the above is "yes."

I do not hesitate to plead guilty to failing to make Jesus' house a house of prayer. Over my many years of ministry, I have wrestled with this dilemma along with my brothers and sisters. Attempts have been made, big pushes have been initiated, prayer meetings have been started, prayer emphases have been introduced into weekend worship services, and much more. But, for many reasons, the impetus behind the pendulum of prayer all too often runs out, and the chime of prayer in the house of God has fallen silent.

Several years ago as I was once again considering Jesus' call that His house be a house of prayer, and wondering how it was ever going to come about, **I felt the Lord say to me, "Since you are my house! You can begin by praying 'Lord make me a house of prayer!'"** It was suddenly as simple and as plain as the image I view in the mirror every morning. He showed me, that as a temple of the Holy Spirit and the dwelling place of God, *I am His house prayer*. In every aspect as His house, I am therefore a key building block or living stone in the house which is His church. **If the church is to become a house of prayer for all nations, it must begin with me!**

That liberated me as I realized that *His* house will be a house of prayer if *I* pray. After several years of praying "Lord, make me a house of prayer," I can now testify that it has revitalized my soul! One of the immediate benefits was that, by God's grace, He began instilling in me a desire to set aside a minimum of one hour every day exclusively to "watch and pray" (Mark 11:14).

Since that time my life has been an ongoing prayer lab. It has been an exciting and educational journey. I have been both relearning and learning for the first time many Biblical principles of prayer. My humble desire is that they will continue to transform me and give my longings for God new life.

Praying "Make me a house of prayer" is one of the most revolutionary and transforming prayers anyone can pray. It is guaranteed to broaden and deepen your prayer life. It will wonderfully draw you into a more intimate relationship with Jesus where He shares His heart with you.

For further meditation and application:

Since God delights in answering prayers that are in line with His will, why not begin to pray "Make me a house of prayer"? I challenge you to pray this prayer daily for 28 days and see what happens.

18

Two Ways to be a
House of Prayer for All Nations

*Is it not written, "My house shall be called a house of prayer
for all nations."* Mark 11:17 NIV

**What did Jesus mean when He said "My house shall be
called a house of prayer for all nations"?** This is a most
critical question. If, as Jesus' teachings and the New
Testament indicate, His "house" over which He is the head
is "the church which is His body," then the church must be
sure to make it a priority to be about that which He has
called it to be (Ephesians 1:22-23; 1Timothy 3:15).

**In order to understand this mandate for the church more
clearly we must look at the context in which Jesus said this
and, specifically, what Hc meant by the phrase "for all
nations."**

**This call for the church to be a house of prayer is recorded
in four separate places in the Scriptures:** three times in the
synoptic Gospels (Matthew 21:13; Mark 11:17; Luke

19:46) and once in Isaiah 56:7 to which Jesus is referring when He says "is it not written." The incident which immediately preceded and triggered this teaching was Jesus' second cleansing of the temple which took place during Passover week prior to His crucifixion.

In His approach to Jerusalem that morning, when He hungered, He came upon a fig tree on which, to His disappointment, He found only leaves and no fruit. His reaction, which startled His disciples, was to curse the tree saying "May no one ever eat fruit from you again!" (Mark 11:14 NIV). **It is commonly understood that the fig tree was representative of the nation of Israel and Jesus' real concern was with Israel's estranged relationship with God His Father.** His burden as He approached the temple was for the spiritual barrenness of His people who should have been bearing the fruit of repentance in turning their hearts toward God.

When He came into the temple and saw the people focused on their own interests by buying and selling, rather than the interests of God by repenting and praying, He was so deeply grieved that He drove the "robbers" out. I tremble to think what the Lord Jesus, who now ever lives to make intercession for us, thinks today as He visits His house of prayer.

It is important to note that the desire of God and His original intention are revealed in the book of Isaiah. There He prophesies that "joy [be] in My house of prayer" where "sacrifices will be accepted," and it will be a "house of prayer for all nations" (Isaiah 56:7 NIV).

What then does it mean to be a "house of prayer for all nations"? The word used here for "nations," both in the Old Testament Hebrew and New Testament Greek passages, literally means peoples, races or nations. It can refer to individual peoples or ethnic groups, as well as governmental and political entities. These references as such are also typically indicating non-Israeli groups. This is significant because the heart of God is revealed here in His all-encompassing love and concern for all peoples, ethnic groups and nations of the earth in addition to Israel. Prophetically, it speaks of His intention to open the door of salvation and redemption to the Gentiles which Paul refers to as the mystery of the ages (Ephesians 3:4-6).

Finally we must examine the words "for all." This phrase is like the treasured final puzzle piece, held in a hand which is poised for placement to complete an intricate picture. It comes from a term meaning "the whole" or "every kind of" and, therefore, describes the all-inclusiveness of the prayer calling.

There are two distinct applications and directives in this phrasing. The first, which seems most obvious from the text, is that God's desire is for all nations to be participants in praying to Him. In other words, the intention of His house of prayer is for it to be a place where *all* belong and *all* have access to God for the purpose of prayer. Furthermore, that intention is that prayer be made *by* all nations.

The second directive of this verse is that all nations or peoples also be the focus of prayer in His house. Stated plainly, His house is to be a place where prayer is not only made *by* all nations, but it is also a place where prayer is made *for* all nations. Since the nations are on God's heart and He watches over the nations (Psalm 66:7), it is clear that prayer in His house must therefore be made *for* all nations.

In order to fulfill Jesus' house-of-prayer command, we must therefore fully embrace the fact that it must be a place of prayer both *by* and *for* all nations! This has so many implications for the Church of Jesus Christ both in terms of the make-up of the church and the focus of the Church's prayer that we will leave all of that for future consideration. **Suffice it to say, let's begin to pray more diligently that His house would become a house of prayer, both *by* and *for* all nations!**

For further meditation and application:

Evaluate your own prayer life and that of your church in terms of being a "house of prayer for all nations." What steps can you take to see this mandate of Jesus fulfilled?

19

Three Reasons for Joy in the House of Prayer

*These I will bring to my holy mountain
and give them joy in my house of prayer.* Isaiah 56:7 NIV

There is something captivating about the promise of joy as a desired end of prayer. Joy is not typically something that we freely associate with prayer – solemnity yes, sobriety, stamina, even anguish, but not joy. But, contrary to conventional wisdom, God is saying in this verse that an accompanying and abiding experience in prayer is meant to be joy.

Practically how does that happen? David, who continually spent time in God's house of prayer, gives us some insight. "You make known to me the *path of life*; in your presence there is *fullness of joy*; at your right hand are *pleasures forevermore*" (Psalm 16:11 NIV *emphasis added*).

From this verse we discover three primary reasons for experiencing joy when we pray.

1. God shares His secrets with us when we pray by giving us a *path of life* revelation. One of the great sources of joy in the place of prayer is the revelation we receive for ourselves and others and the direction in which to pray. Jeremiah puts it this way "Call to me and I will answer you and tell you great and unsearchable things you do not know" (Jeremiah 33:3 NIV).

2. When we pray God promises His presence and the *fullness of joy* that accompanies His presence. The essence of that joy is simply spending time with Him. It is in getting to know Him, His nature and character, and His ways. Moses, who experienced God's presence as few men, cried out to God, "If you are pleased with me, teach me your ways so I may know you and continue to find favor with you" (Exodus 33:13 NIV).

3. We have the *pleasure* and privilege of exercising Kingdom authority when we pray. The right hand of God is where Christ is seated in heavenly places, far above all rule and authority; it is there in the Spirit we are seated with Him (Ephesians 2:6). From a place of prayer, we enter into non-stop intercession with Jesus so that "His name be hallowed, His kingdom come and His will be done on earth as it is in heaven." I believe that "the pleasures forevermore" at the Father's right hand are the sense of purpose and accomplishment we feel when we are making a difference in the world through our intercession with Jesus.

Like many people, I can personally confirm that there is a remarkable release of joy when entering into a season of concentrated prayer. Such joy is typically not attendant to the casual or intermittent pray-er, but reserved for those who, with diligence, set their hearts to seek the Lord with regularity over extended periods of time. Believe me, I have learned this by experience. This is not to say that God will not break in with His joy upon anyone who prays under any condition, for God is sovereign, but the abiding experience of joy comes most readily to those who abide in His presence.

As I think about the times in prayer when I have been overcome with joy, it has invariably been a result of one or more of the three causes of joy listed above. God has given me joy in His house of prayer when I've heard His voice, sensed His manifest presence, and/or felt the anointing to make a throne room proclamation of His will. In those times, I can certainly identify with Joshua when he chose to stay in the Lord's presence rather than accompany Moses back to the camp (Exodus 33:11). I want to linger in His presence myself and let the rest of the world go by.

For further meditation and application:

When was the last time you were filled with joy by being in the presence of God? What were the circumstances surrounding that encounter? Take time to thank God right now for His faithfulness to reveal Himself and encourage you in such a precious way. Look with expectancy toward more joy-filled experiences in His presence.

20

The Call to Pray for the Nations

Ask me, and I will make the nations your inheritance,
the ends of the earth your possession. Psalm 2:8 NIV

It is hard to comprehend what a magnanimous heart God has when one considers the verse "For God so loved the world that He gave His one and only Son, that whoever believes in Him shall not perish but have eternal life" (John 3:16 NIV). Think about it - the *world*. The entire world includes nearly 200 nations and the 7 billion people who inhabit them. That takes a whole lot of love, something only Jesus could accomplish through His death on the cross, burial, and resurrection. And it is His ultimate intention that "all the nations, whom [He] has made shall come and worship before [Him]" (Psalm 86:9 NASB).

Even a cursory reading of the Bible immediately conveys this loving concern God carries for the nations of the world. We are explicitly told in Psalm 66 that "His eyes keep watch on the nations" (vs. 7). In nearly every book of the Bible, we find the evidence of this heart expressed through prophetic utterances and/or divine initiatives to both reveal

Himself and draw nations toward Himself through repentance and faith. From His Old Testament promise to Abraham to bless all the nations of the world through him, to the New Testament command of Jesus that the gospel of the kingdom be proclaimed throughout the entire world, we see His unshakeable purpose to make the nations His inheritance (Genesis 22:18; Matthew 24:14). Again, that is a whole lot of love! How can He possibly do that?

His choice is to do it through the instrumentation of prayer and intercession. From the book of Genesis forward, we find God looking for individuals to answer His call to become intercessors on behalf of His purposes for the nations. Just consider the intercessory ministries of the likes of Noah, Moses, Daniel, Nehemiah, the prophets, Paul, and the apostles. "Ask of me, and I will make the nations your inheritance" He pleads (Psalm 2:8 NIV). "I looked for someone among them who would build up the wall and stand before me in the gap on behalf of the land so I would not have to destroy it, but I found no one," He declares through Ezekiel (22:30 NIV). "He saw that there was no man, and wondered that there was no one to intercede; then His own arm brought Him salvation, and His righteousness upheld Him" (Isaiah 59:16 ESV). And with that He calls forth His son Jesus who alone is able to save and who "ever lives to make intercession" (Hebrews 7:25 AKJV).

Intercession, which is building up a wall of protection against the enemy and standing in the gap before God on behalf of human kind, is God's chosen way of initiating His will in the earth (Ezekiel 22:30). That is why Jesus urges us to pray "thy kingdom come, thy will be done on earth as it is in heaven" (Matthew 6:10 KJV).

Intercession is God's invitation to His people, His church, to be co-workers together with Him in the business of governing the world. This truth is underscored by one of the last public messages Jesus gave the week before He died when His stated plainly His call to intercession for the nations: "My house shall be called a house of prayer for all nations!" (Mark 11:17 ESV). This explains why we are told through the revelation of Paul that "God raised us up with Christ and seated us with Him in the heavenly realms in Christ Jesus" (Ephesians 2:6 NIV). Just imagine, He has given us a place in the Spirit where, when yielded and unified with the enthroned Christ, we can actually rule and reign with Him from a place of prayer. You can read more on this in the Chapter 5, *What it means to pray with Jesus.*

Since intercessory prayer for the nations is so important and so strategic for the fulfillment of God's purposes, why then is there so little of it being made in the Church? Since it is so near and dear to God's heart, why then are we not more committed to doing it? Could it be that, like the money changers and merchants in the temple, we have become more concerned with our own profit and well-being than with the spiritual well-being of the nations?

Intercession is God's love expressed in prayer from our knees. There is something about praying for the nations that taps us into God's heart of love. I know of no other way to explain it. We find ourselves lifted out of the narrowness of self into the heights and depths of His love for His creation. As we begin to fathom the mystery of God's holiness and justice we find ourselves pleading with Him for His mercy and compassion based on His steadfast love and faithfulness.

I believe there is a unique and inherent blessing for those individuals, families and corporate groups (ministries and churches) who make it a priority to regularly intercede for the nations. It is directly tied to the simple principle that if we give preference to the things that concern God, He will be sure to give preference to the things that concern us. It is directly in line with the great promise "Seek first the kingdom of God and His righteousness and all these things will be given to you as well" (Matthew 6:33 ESV).

For further meditation and application:

If you are praying "Make me a house of prayer" why not add "for all nations"? Begin to pray Psalm 2:8 asking God to burden you for at least one nation in addition to the United States. Add that nation to your list of mandates for you pray regularly.

21

Look at the Nations and Watch!

Look at the nations and watch-- and be utterly amazed. For I am going to do something in your days that you would not believe, even if you were told.
Habakkuk 1:5 NIV

"Look at the nations and watch!" This is as timely an exhortation today as it was over 2500 years ago when it was first given! Keeping a watchful eye on what is happening in the nations is critical because Jesus commanded us that, as His people, we engage in being a house of prayer for *all nations*. Watching the nations provides us with understanding into the unfolding of God's purposes in the earth. It also arms us with strategic insights into ways in which we can intercede for His kingdom to come and His will to be done on earth as it is in heaven.

The manner in which the nations relate to God and His people, both Israel and the church, has always been associated with the blessings or judgments that He metes out. The three-chapter book of Habakkuk provides an excellent illustration of how God invites us, through intercession, into His history-shaping intervention in the nations.

Habakkuk was a prophet in the years preceding the fall of Jerusalem in 586 BC and the resultant Jewish exile. It was at a time when God was raising up the Babylonians to bring judgment upon Judea and the surrounding nations for their lawlessness and injustice (Habakkuk 1:6-17). **What Habakkuk saw happening in the nations caused him to take a stand before God as a watchman intercessor (2:1).** In so doing, he was seeking to understand what God was doing and to intercede on behalf of God's people and purposes in the earth. "Lord," he prayed, "I have heard of your fame; I stand in awe of your deeds, Lord. Repeat them, in our time make them known; in wrath remember mercy" (3:2 NIV).

This is a common pattern throughout the Bible, particularly in the lives of the prophets, when God took initiative to reveal to His servants what He was doing among the nations and call them to intercession (Isaiah 59:16; Ezekiel 22:30). Not surprisingly, God's strategic dealings with the nations continue to this day! This call to "look at the nations and watch – and be utterly amazed" is even more relevant for us today "upon whom the end of the ages has come" (1 Corinthians 10:11 ESV).

There are seven billion people on the planet, making up over 16,000 distinct people groups who speak roughly 6500 languages and inhabit nearly 200 politically defined nations. They are all people whom God loves and for whom He sent His son Jesus to die and redeem.

What happens in those nations governmentally, religiously, educationally, economically, militarily, in the arts, entertainment and media affects the advancement or restriction of the gospel and ultimately their salvation. How they relate to other nations, the church, Israel, and, most importantly, to God, determines their place in God's end-time destiny. It is He who controls the course of world events, and it is He who will have the last word. "He changes times and seasons; he deposes kings and raises up others. He gives wisdom to the wise and knowledge to the discerning" (Daniel 2:21 NIV).

Given these facts, what then should we watch for as we look at the nations? Here are five things in the form of questions we should ask about the nations that will help us intercede.

1. How do they relate to the church of Jesus Christ? Is there freedom to worship and preach the gospel? Or are believers restricted in their activities and even persecuted for their faith? Is the church merely surviving or is it thriving?

2. How do they relate to Israel? There are clear promises in Scripture that those who bless Israel will themselves be blessed and those who curse it will be cursed (Genesis 12:3). What nations are friendly to Israel and what nations oppose her?

3. How do they relate to those who are victims of injustice? How do their domestic and foreign policies affect the poor, the weak and vulnerable, the minorities, those suffering, the refugee, the widow and orphan?

4. Where does it appear that anti-Christ principalities and powers are forming battle lines in the spiritual realm? Where are there shifts in power? Which nations are extending their influence and dominion? What nations are losing their influence and control – and to whom? How and with whom are nations aligned economically, politically, and/or militarily?

5. Where is God at work in and through all these things? Can you see what God is doing to extend His kingdom and the righteousness of which He has promised an increase without end?

I have personally found these observations very helpful in praying for God's purposes to unfold in the nations. God has a way of combining our natural understanding with spiritual revelation that leads to anointed, energized times of intercession (1 Corinthians 14:15). Being "utterly amazed" at what God is doing is often the result.

For further meditation and application:

Is God stirring your heart in this dimension of prayer? How has God led you in answering Jesus' call to be a house of prayer for all nations?

22

How to Pray for the Nations

And as He taught them, He said, "Is it not written: 'My house will be called a house of prayer for all nations'?"
Mark 11:17 & Isaiah 56:7 NIV

While Jesus' call to pray for the nations of the world is indisputable, the practical how-tos of such a momentous task are not as clear. Praying effectively for the nations requires digging into both Old and New Testament Scriptures to discern God's ultimate purposes for the nations.

Because we know that the key to getting our prayers heard and answered is to pray according to His will, we must ask the question: what is God's will with regard to the nations of the world? "This is the confidence we have in approaching God: that if we ask anything according to his will, he hears us. And if we know that he hears us--whatever we ask--we know that we have what we asked of him" (1 John 5:14-15 NIV).

From a study of the Bible, the following are five ways, the

ABCDE's, in which to pray for any given nation based on God's will and His ways in dealing with the nations.

A. Authorities - Pray for the leaders of nations – In one of the seminal calls to intercession for governmental leaders Paul writes "I urge, then, first of all, that petitions, prayers, intercession and thanksgiving be made for all people—for kings (presidents, prime ministers, dictators etc.) and all those in authority, that we may live peaceful and quiet lives in all godliness and holiness" (1 Timothy 2:1-2 NIV). It helps to keep in mind that God can sovereignly work in a leader's life and make a way where there seems to be no way. Nothing is too hard for Him (Proverbs 21:1; Isaiah 43:19; Jeremiah 32:27). Pray for the gift of good government and for God to change times and seasons in nations by deposing bad rulers and raising up wise and righteous ones (Psalm 75:5-7; Daniel 2:21).

B. Believers - Pray for the believers and churches in that country – God's purposes on earth are ordained to be accomplished through His church. In Jesus' great prayer for His followers recorded in John 17, we have a perfect model to use in praying for believers in a nation. There we see Him praying for the church to be 1) Glorifying God (17:1; 4), 2) Fortified against the enemy (17:11; 12; 15), 3) Unified (17:11; 21-23), 4) Sanctified (17:17; 19), 5) Multiplied (17:18; 20-21), 6) Filled with Joy (17:13), and 7) Seeing His Glory (17:24).

The Bible also encourages us to remember those who are persecuted for their faith and suffering as though we ourselves were there with them. (Hebrews 13:3) Therefore it is important to pray that God would bless them with His presence, comfort them, and deliver them (Matthew 5:10;

Psalm 139:8; 2 Corinthians 1:3-4; Psalm 72:12-14).

C. Contrition - Pray prayers of repentant confession on behalf of the nation – "Righteousness exalts a nation, but sin condemns any people" (Proverbs 14:34 NIV). God's dealings with the nations, as demonstrated primarily in the Old Testament, were always based upon their relationship with Him and the corresponding obedience or disobedience to His moral law summed up in the Ten Commandments. He was continually appealing to them through His prophets to return to Him with humility and repentance, acknowledging their sin and asking for His mercy. Seek to identify in prayer the strongholds ruling over the nation that keep its people in bondage, and then pray that they might be torn down and the captives set free (2 Corinthians 10:4; Matthew 16:19, 18:18).

The role of the intercessor is to confess on behalf of the nation their sins, asking for God's forgiveness, appealing to His mercy, and reminding Him of His ultimate purposes for that nation. Two excellent models that can be used for such a prayer are the great intercessory prayers made by Moses and Nehemiah on behalf of the nation of Israel (Deuteronomy 9:26-29; Nehemiah 1:4-11).

D. Destiny - Pray for each nation to fulfill God's destiny – God's ultimate intention is that every nation will one day worship and glorify Him. In the book of Revelation we see a glimpse of a heavenly host singing what is referred to as the "song of Moses and of the Lamb" in which they declare, "All nations will come and worship before you, for your righteous acts have been revealed" (Revelation 15:4 NIV). This is a direct quote from Psalm 86:9 which concludes with "they will bring glory to your name." What an amazing picture this paints of God's unrelenting purpose that "the kingdom of this world [becomes] the kingdom of our Lord, and of His Christ" that He might reign forever and ever (Revelation 11:15 ESV).

Each nation in its founding was birthed with spiritual DNA for the establishment of the Kingdom of God. Discovering God's original intent for a nation by studying its history is therefore a worthwhile pursuit. It enables the intercessor to pray with conviction for the fulfillment of His divine purposes for that nation. "Listen to me, you who pursue righteousness and who seek the LORD: Look to the rock from which you were cut and to the quarry from which you were hewn" (Isaiah 51:1 NIV).

E. Evangelism - Pray for the unfettered preaching of the Gospel – Jesus' last command, known as the Great Commission, was for His followers to go forth into the *whole* world to *all* nations in order to preach the gospel of the kingdom and make disciples (Matthew 24:14, Mark 13:10). Practically, that means praying for God to raise up Gospel workers to go forth into the harvest fields and for the effective and bold witness, even in the face of persecution, of all believers, both citizens and foreigners, in a given country (Matthew 9:38). Paul the Apostle makes it plain with regard to the nations that God "wants all people to be saved and come to a knowledge of the truth" (I Timothy 2:3 NIV).

Pray both with the spirit and with the understanding – There are basically two approaches a person can take in praying for something or someone. We can pray by revelation from the Holy Spirit and by understanding we have gained from acquired knowledge. Paul encourages intercessors to do both. "What am I to do? I will pray with my spirit, but I will also pray with my understanding (mind)" (1 Corinthians 14:15 ESV). It is important to always be dependent upon the Holy Spirit for revelation in our praying, sensing both the focus of our prayer and specifically how to pray. But there is also a great benefit in gathering information about the subject of our prayer that provides wisdom in praying with greater depth of understanding. When combining revelation and research, invariably we find both a deepening of our burden and quickening of our faith.

An invaluable tool to use in praying for the nations is a recently updated version of *Operation World*, an amazing book subtitled a *Definitive Prayer Guide for Every Nation.* It provides background and statistical information on each country's geography, people, economy, politics, and religion plus answers to and challenges for prayer. In addition, **a person can do research on key nations** using the internet and also subscribe to daily Google news alerts for countries of interest to get daily news articles on developing trends.

This list of approaches in praying for the nations is by no means exhaustive or definitive, but it can provide a good starting place in answering Jesus' call to be a house of prayer for all nations.

For further meditation and application:

Pause now and think of a nation for which God has given you a burden in prayer. Using this ABCDE outline as a way to pray, spend some time praying for your nation of choice. After you are finished, evaluate ways in which using the outline was beneficial in your prayer time. Make a commitment to applying what you have learned in your future prayers for the nations.

23

Making Your Church a House of Prayer

Poverty-stricken as the Church is today in many things, she is most stricken here, in the place of prayer. We have many organizers, but few agonizers; many players and payers, few pray-ers; many singers, few clingers; lots of pastors, few wrestlers; many fears, few tears; much fashion, little passion; many interferers, few intercessors; many writers, but few fighters. Failing here, we fail everywhere.[1]
Leonard Ravenhill

This diagnosis of the sad state of the church with regard to prayer, though penned over fifty years ago, is as accurate today as it was then. The quote above is taken from Leonard Ravenhill's 1959 classic, *Why Revival Tarries*. It is both unfathomable and disheartening to consider that the one declared priority of Jesus for His Church, that it be a house of prayer, has continued over the years to be so mindlessly disregarded.

This is particularly true of evangelical churches in the West. Lip service is typically given to prayer by it being relegated to a brief invocation of God's blessing upon the worship service, the offering, and/or the message. In the average church service, the percentage of actual time given to prayer is woefully small in comparison to time spent in singing, preaching, fellowshipping, and even the announcements. No sustained and focused prayer is devoted to the broad spectrum of need in the Church, the community, and the world.

Prayer in the church is a lot like the weather. Mark Twain once said, "Everybody talks about the weather, but nobody does anything about it." That same thing could be said about prayer. There is more talking about it in the church than actually doing it. What will it take for churches to give as much or more priority to being houses of prayer than houses of preaching, worship, fellowship, or Sunday school?

It is important to note that those churches rooted in a liturgical tradition are much better at making prayer a priority in their services than contemporary churches. Prayer is woven into the fabric of centuries-old traditions of interceding for a plethora of needs both within and without the church. It provides a continual reminder and example of the priority of both corporate and private prayer.

The dirty little secret about establishing a culture of prayer in the church is that its implementation depends upon the pastor. Nothing will change the prayerlessness of a church without the pastor taking the lead. It is he, and he alone, who must see that prayer is established as a priority and will be carried out come hell or high water. Others may take the initiative to pray for a pastor and encourage him to make prayer the priority in the church, but the actual implementation can only be done by him.

Being a member of a prayer-less church that lacks a pastor to lead the charge in prayer is not, however, a hopeless situation. Individuals who are convinced that prayer makes a difference can covenant together to pray for their pastor and encourage him in appropriate ways to implement prayer as a priority in the church. In addition, for any pastor or church leader reading this, you can begin by praying for yourself asking that Jesus would make *you* a house of prayer. See Chapter 17, *Make Me a House of Prayer*.

The best news of all is that there are some very practical things that, under the leadership of its pastor, every church can do to remedy this prayer malaise. I have discovered from years of pastoring congregations and gleaning wisdom from others that **there are three key ingredients for establishing a culture of prayer in a church. For simplicity's sake they can be summarized with 3 M's: Mandates, Modeling, and Mobilization.**

1. MANDATES – **Just as individual pray-ers are encouraged to discern their personal prayer mandates from God (people and things for which they are called to pray), steps need to be taken on a corporate level to establish church-wide mandates.** (See Chapter 15, *The Why and How of Prayer Mandates*.) Defining the specific prayer burdens which God lays upon a church not only becomes a rallying point for prayer, but also establishes an ongoing commitment to corporately persevere to see that prayer answered.

The pastor and leadership team of each local church should seek the Lord to identify and define five to seven key strategic focal points for prayer in their church. These will become their church's prayer mandates. These mandates should include such things as: congregational needs and prayer requests, the church and its ministries, the community and its subcultures, state and federal needs, current events, selected nations of the world, Israel, justice issues, the persecuted church, and suffering of the world etc.

In practice, leaders should keep their prayer mandates before their congregations by regularly publishing and praying for them. Days of the week may be assigned to each mandate and weekly or monthly time devoted at public gatherings, especially on Sundays, to praying for them. Periodically throughout the year, a focused emphasis on individual mandates may also be initiated. One way to do this is by scheduling special meetings featuring guest speakers with expertise on a given mandate.

2. MODELING – The maxim "things are better caught than taught" aptly applies to the challenge of encouraging and teaching people how to pray. Jesus knew this and demonstrated repeatedly that modeling a life of prayer whetted His disciples' appetite to pray and motivated them to want to pray in like manner. Wise pastors and church leaders would do well to follow in Jesus' footsteps by taking advantage at every opportunity to model prayer before the congregation. They should define the venues (services, meetings, gatherings) and ways (formats, means) in which they will commit to consistently modeling a culture of prayer focused on their church's God-given mandates.

The most logical and critical place to begin modeling prayer is in the Sunday service(s). It is the only meeting in the week which everyone attends with any regularity. Consequently, it has the greatest potential for impact and must therefore become a pastor's highest priority for modeling prayer in the congregation. If a pastor is going to develop a culture of prayer in the church, he must begin here!

Practically speaking, I would recommend that a pastor start by setting aside a minimum of ten minutes in the Sunday service to devote to prayer. To those who balk at this length of time, consider this: "Who are we out to please?" Unquestionably it is God, for He has declared that "the prayer of the upright is His delight" (Proverbs 15:8 NASB). Lest we forget, not only are we pleasing Him, but we are also richly blessing those who are the focus and the recipients of our prayers. In regards to the congregation, careful and prayerful planning by the leaders will go a long way toward creating an engaging prayer time. The use of varying formats from week to week, coupled with a changing focus on the different mandates, will cause the time to fly by.

3. MOBILIZATION – The secret to birthing the prayer ministry of a church is to mobilize those people who already have a calling and passion for prayer. As intercessors and prayer warriors they are the engine that will drive prayer ministry and the key to growing a culture of prayer. Intercessors, like evangelists, typically represent about ten percent of a church's membership. It is important that church leadership make a commitment to caring for and fueling this engine if it hopes to see the prayer ministries of the church prosper.

Church leaders should begin by deciding the specific prayer ministries they want the church to have and develop an overall plan for launching and maintaining them. They can then initiate a process of identifying all those in the church who have a burden for prayer and invite them to come together for a special meeting. The purpose of this meeting should be twofold: to create an environment of appreciation and encouragement for all the faithful prayer warriors *and* to give them a vision of the possibilities of developing a culture of prayer in the church. Underscoring the importance of their roles in growing the prayer ministry of the church is paramount. The beginnings of prayer leadership for the various prayer ministries of the church should wisely be drawn from this group. Also, keep in mind that these precious saints will naturally become the prime influencers to spark the participation of others as various prayer ministries begin.

Diagnoses are often hard to take, but finding the right remedy to an affliction engenders hope. My desire is that the remedy offered here to Ravenhill's diagnosis of the prayer-less church offers hope to you in your church situation. I dream of the day when every local church is truly a house of prayer, where there are more agonizers than organizers, more pray-ers than players or payers, more clingers than singers, more intercessors than interferers. Will you join me in dreaming – and praying?

For further meditation and application:

How would Ravenhill describe your church? Be as specific as you can. What remedy, if necessary, would you prescribe? Are you one of the ten percent in your church who has a gifting and calling for prayer? How might God be directing you to be a catalyst in your church to promote a culture of prayer?

1. Leonard Ravenhill, Why Revival Tarries, (Minneapolis, MN: Bethany House, 1959, 1987), 25.

24

The Watchman Calling

Could you not watch with me one hour? Watch and pray that you may not enter into temptation. The spirit indeed is willing, but the flesh is weak. Matthew 26:40-41 ESV

Watching and praying, or what the Bible refers to as being a spiritual "watchman," may be the most critically important aspect of prayer that there is. The very nature of being a watchman requires an alertness and vigilance to impending danger. It demands taking the appropriate steps of obedience of faith to either stop it, avoid it, or prepare to endure it. Jesus' challenge to His disciples in the garden of Gethsemane to "watch and pray" illustrates this truth like none other. His agony expressed in prayer was directly linked to His *watching* to see what His Father was showing Him and His obedient response. Tragically, His disciples were sleeping instead of watching and praying. As a result, they found themselves unprepared for what was about to unfold. Unfortunately, it is an all too familiar portrait of the condition of most churches today with regard to watchful prayer.

The call to the watchman prayer ministry has its roots in the Old Testament. In ancient times, the function of the watchmen was to position themselves by continuous shifts in strategic perches upon a wall or tower in order to guard a city by scanning the distance for anything or anyone approaching. In addition to looking and listening, their responsibility was to give a warning of any approaching danger while urging the appropriate action be taken to protect and defend the city.

Through the prophets Isaiah and Ezekiel, God Himself made urgent appeals, just as Jesus did in the garden, for His people to post spiritual watchmen. "Go, set a watchman; let him announce what he sees. . . let him listen diligently, very diligently" (Isaiah 21:6 ESV). "But if the watchman sees the sword coming and does not blow the trumpet to warn the people . . . I will hold the watchman accountable for their blood" (Ezekiel 33:6 NIV). That is a sobering thought and readily applicable to the watchman prayer ministry, as life or death may literally be held in the balance.

Is it any wonder that in the New Testament, beginning with the teachings of Jesus and carrying through in the writings of the apostles, we see repeated calls to be watchful, sober, and vigilant unto prayer? In many cases the appeals are concerning the evil days in which we live, God's judgments, and the imminence of the end times. Peter sums it up well when he writes, "The end of all things is near. Therefore be alert and of sober mind so that you may pray" (1 Peter 4:7 NIV).

The key role of a prayer watchman is best described by the words "intercede" or "intercession." To intercede means to position oneself between two entities and to interpose on behalf of one, which is just like the role of a watchman on the wall.

The best Biblical definition of this type of prayer is found in Ezekiel 22:30 which describes God's desperate search for a watchman intercessor. "I looked for someone among them who would *build up the wall and stand before me in the gap* on behalf of the land so I would not destroy it, but I found no one" (NIV *emphasis added*).

Here we have a graphic picture of a watchman's call both to "build up the wall" of defense against an enemy and to "stand before [God] in the gap" on behalf of someone or something. That is prayer at its quintessential best - a picture of the watchman intercessor's highest call to put himself or herself on the line both in defense against an enemy and in an appeal before God on behalf of the one being defended. That is what Jesus willingly chose to do on the cross, as a result of His watching and praying in the garden. In defense of a sinful world deserving judgment and under the power of the evil one, He took his place upon the cross as that intercessor for whom God was looking in Ezekiel 22:30. His substitutionary death defended us once and for all, from both the wrath of a just God against sin and the control of the devil who held the power of death.

The call to watchman intercession is a call to watch and pray in the same spirit as our Savior. It is a call to put our lives on the line, in prayer, for someone or something earnestly appealing to God on their behalf while also

fiercely defending them from the spiritual attacks of the enemy of their souls. There are many illustrations of this critical ministry throughout the Bible. Abraham interceded before God in an actual bargaining exchange on behalf of his nephew Lot who lived in wicked Sodom which was slated for judgment (Genesis 18). Both Moses and the Apostle Paul were so earnest in their prayer for Israel's salvation that they offered their very lives in exchange (Exodus 32:31; Romans 9:1-5; 10:1).

For further meditation and application:

Do the words of Jesus "could you not watch with me one hour" stir something deep within your heart? If so, give some thought to practical steps you can take in response? If you feel called to be a watchman on God's intercession wall, seek out others with a similar calling with whom you can fellowship and pray.

25

Four Things Every Watchman Must Do

I will stand at my watch post; I will remain stationed on the city wall. I will keep watching, so I can see what he says to me and can know how I should answer when he counters my argument. Habakkuk 2:1 NET

The ministry of a watchman is a form of prayer that is focused on praying for God's purposes and protection over a specific people, geographical area, and/or nation. It requires dedication, focus, consistency, and perseverance. The watchman's passion is to discern the will of God and pray it into existence. Simply put, the watchman is called to watch and pray. While everyone is commanded in the Scriptures to be sober, vigilant, and watchful for the purpose of prayer, not everyone has a specific calling and gifting to be a watchman.

Those with a watchman calling could be likened to the person standing next to a wall who is graced with sufficient stature to simply look over the wall for prolonged views of the other side. For those without such stature, extra effort is required with a leap or a ladder for even a limited view.

However, regardless of anyone's calling, it is beneficial for all of us, watchmen and non-watchmen alike, to consider how to grow and function more effectively in the watching and praying ministry.

Here then, from a Biblical overview, are the four essential functions of the prayer ministry of the watchman. An effective watchman is engaged in . . .

1. WAITING upon the Lord. The overarching posture of the watchman, and his or her first priority, is always to wait upon the Lord. **The waiting process is marked primarily by looking and listening to discern what God is saying.** The prophet Habakkuk, himself a watchman, described it this way: "I will stand at my watch post; I will remain stationed on the city wall. I will keep watching, *so I can see what he says to me* and can know how I should answer when he counters my argument" (NET *emphasis added*).

Waiting is often associated with worship. "Praise awaits you, our God in Zion" (Psalm 65:1 NIV). Worship invites God's presence, and with His presence comes the release of His revelation to the watchman's heart. The Lord, through the prophet Isaiah, *"let him listen diligently, very diligently"* (Isaiah 21:7 ESV *emphasis added*). That, in a nutshell, is the best advice a watchman can get!

2. WRITING down what the Lord is revealing, both for reflection and future action. This is the one aspect of watching that is probably most overlooked. The Lord spoke specifically to Habakkuk, as He would to all of us regarding revelation that He gives: "**Write down this message! Record it legibly on tablets,** so the one who announces it may read it easily" (Habakkuk 2:1 NET *emphasis added*). Thank God for all the prophets and scribes of both the Old and New Testaments who had the presence of mind to faithfully record what God was saying and doing.

God is still speaking today, and we would do well to record the things He reveals to us as we watch and wait for Him. A written record allows time for reflection and further discernment as to how to pray. It also provides space to consider if God is giving direction for some specific action steps of faith that need to be taken.

3. WRESTLING *with* **God for His purposes to be established in the earth and** *against* **demonic powers hindering the way.** Isaiah gives us insight into the persistence in prayer that is expected of watchmen by the Lord. "I have posted watchmen on your walls, Jerusalem; *they will never be silent day or night.* You who call on the LORD, *give yourselves no rest, and give him no rest* till he establishes Jerusalem and makes her the praise of the earth" (Isaiah 62:6-7 NIV *emphasis added*). Like Jacob wrestling with the angel, we as watchmen are to show the same tenacity in not letting go until He blesses (Genesis 32:22-32).

By the same token, as watchman like Daniel, we must relentlessly wrestle "against the rulers, against the authorities, against the cosmic powers over this present darkness, *against the spiritual forces of evil in the heavenly places*" until the enemy is defeated and the victory is won (Ephesians 6:12 ESV *emphasis added*; Daniel 10).

4. WARNING, when necessary, at the prompting of the Lord. Sometimes spiritual watchmen, like natural ones, are responsible before the Lord to issue a warning. Several times in the book of Ezekiel we see God telling him, "Son of man, I have made you a watchman for the people of Israel; *so hear the word I speak and give them warning* from me" (Ezekiel 3:17; 33:7 NIV *emphasis added*).

One caveat here would be that warnings should be given in the fear of the Lord and only after earnest waiting, writing and wrestling. The watchman should have, as Ezekiel did, a clear word from the Lord to take what God has shown in prayer and share it appropriately. Cultivating a healthy fear of the Lord is the best way to insure God's wisdom as to how to steward the revelation that He gives (Proverbs 9:10).

For further meditation and application:

As you consider the four aspects of the watchman ministry, which one(s) would you most like to experience growth and greater effectiveness, in your prayer life? What steps can you take to realize that desire?

26

The Mark of an Intercessor

He said to him, "Walk through the streets of Jerusalem and
put a mark on the foreheads of all who weep and sigh
because of the detestable sins being committed in their city."
Ezekiel 9:4 NLT

God takes special note of those who share in the grief of His heart for the sinful world around them. As in every generation throughout history, there are many things today that vex the souls of God-fearing people, just as they did the righteous soul of Lot in his day (2 Peter 2:4-9). We are being inundated by an unending flood of evil, the news of which, like a deluge, is coming from every corner of the world, streaming day and night through multiple forms of media.

Ezekiel, while in captivity in Babylon, is visited by God and taken in the Spirit to the temple in Jerusalem. There he is shown, among other things, God's preparation to bring judgment on the city. He sees six men appear, each with a deadly weapon in their hands, and he sees with them a man clothed in linen with a writing kit at his side. Then he hears God call to the linen clad man and instruct to him to "walk through the streets of Jerusalem and put a mark on the foreheads of all who weep and sigh because of the detestable sins being committed in their city." In startling succession, the next two verses contain the instructions given to six other men. They are told to "Follow him through the city and kill, without showing pity or compassion . . . but do not touch anyone who has the mark" (Ezekiel 9:5-6 NIV).

What caused God to mark these people for mercy rather than for judgment? We are told that they were weeping and sighing because of the sinfulness of the city.

It is instructive here to look at the root meanings of these two words. The Hebrew word for "weep" conveys the type of crying associating with lament or mourning. This indicates that these people were genuinely grieving the condition of the society around them. The Hebrew word for "sigh" means to exhale, to moan, and to groan. This is particularly insightful because, in the New Testament, Spirit-led and inspired intercession is referred to in exactly the same way. "Likewise the Spirit helps us in our weakness. For we do not know what to pray for as we ought, but the Spirit himself intercedes for us with groanings too deep for words" (Romans 8:26 ESV).

In fact, we even see Jesus interceding at the tomb of Lazarus "with groanings too deep for words." When He encounters Mary and the other Jews weeping with her, we are told "He groaned in the spirit, and was troubled" (John 11:33 KJV).

Again let's ask the question – what caused God to take special note of these people and mark them as recipients of

His mercy? I am of the firm conviction that it was a direct result of them entering into and carrying a spirit of intercession for the sinful world around them. I believe that the weeping and sighing going on in the spirits of these people was Holy Spirit-inspired prayer and intercession. The manner in which they were sharing the grief of the heart of God, through intercession for His creation, so deeply pleased Him that He extended His scepter of mercy even in the midst of His judgments to spare them.

I find this passage of scripture a great encouragement with regard to the ministry of intercession. It underscores the fact that being an intercessor who pleases and touches the heart of God is more about the why of intercession than the how. It is more about why we groan than how we groan, more about being than overtly doing or even saying anything. Ultimately, it is about who we allow ourselves to become as we yield to Him and increasingly identify with His grief for the world.

The ministry of intercession, at its very core is identifying with God. It is a state of being from which naturally flows weeping and sighing for His creation.

For further meditation and application:

Have you had the experience during times of prayer, when you found yourself drawn into a state of groaning and/or weeping? Did it seem like you were sensing the heart of God for those whom you were praying? If so, it may be an indication that God has marked you as an intercessor. Ask God to help you to become more and more yielded to the Holy Spirit for Him to pray through you in this way.

27

Two Things that Amaze God

Why Intercession is so Important to God

Have you wondered if God is ever amazed? If so, what kind of things do you think amaze Him?

In my searching of the Scriptures, I have found only two times where we are literally told that God had that kind of reaction to something. One is in the Old Testament, and one is recorded in the New Testament gospels.

It is significant to note that in both cases, God's amazement or astonishment was related to the issue of intercession. Intercession as Biblically defined is a type of prayer, often followed up by action, that protects someone in peril by making "up a hedge and stand[ing] in the gap before" God on their behalf (Ezekiel 22:30 KJV). In Chapter 29: *Praying a Hedge of Protection*, this aspect of intercession is explained in greater detail.

Here are the only two times recorded when God is amazed:

1. When He Cannot Find an Intercessor! - The prophet Isaiah, in chapter 59, is recounting the iniquitous condition of Israel and the fact that no one is calling for justice or pleading their case with integrity, i.e., interceding (vs. 2-4). In recounting their sin, he finally declares, "The Lord saw it, and it displeased Him that there was no justice. He saw that there was no man, and wondered (literally was "amazed" or "astonished") that there was no one to intercede; then His own arm brought Him salvation, and His righteousness upheld Him" (15b-16 ESV).

We know from this passage that Isaiah is speaking prophetically of the coming of Jesus, the Messiah, who would willingly suffer a substitutionary death for the salvation of the world, and who now ever lives to make intercession (Hebrews 7:25).

2. When He Finds a Faith-Filled Intercessor! – In Jesus' encounter with the Roman Centurion who came to Him on behalf of his servant, we see the only other time in Scripture where God is amazed. In this case, a non-Jew comes to Jesus interceding with these simple words of faith: "just say the word and my servant will be healed" (Luke 7:7 NIV). After the centurion proceeds to explain his understanding of how authority works, Jesus "was amazed at him and turning to the crowd following Him said 'I tell you, I have not found such great faith, even in Israel'" (Luke 7:9 NIV).

There is a valuable lesson to be learned from these two illustrations of God's amazement. This side of the cross, it is not only preferable, but also possible, to amaze God more by our intercession than by our lack thereof. The fact is that, through the cross, Jesus appeased the Father's amazement for the want of an intercessor, as recorded in Isaiah. That appeasement now enables and empowers all of us who are recipients of His redemptive grace to amaze Him instead by becoming faith-filled intercessors ourselves.

Not unlike the centurion, each of us as believers has the great privilege to come to Him daily in prayer, interceding with authority on behalf of others. In so doing, we, like the centurion, can cause Jesus to marvel at our intercession and be expectant for His answers to be released.

For further meditation and application:

May I encourage you to avoid amazing God for the wrong reason by seeking to amaze Him for the right reason? Since intercession is so pleasing and important to God, how might you begin to incorporate more of it in your life?

.

28

Intercession - Love on its Knees

Expressing our Love for Others from a Place of Prayer

Most Christians would agree that demonstrating a self-sacrificial love for others is the essence of the gospel message and the highest form of obedience we can render to the New Commandment of Jesus. Our common concept of expressing Christ's love is typically associated with our feet (going), our hands (serving), and our mouths (proclaiming). **But how often do we associate His love as being expressed from our knees through praying?**

We think of love, and rightly so, as an action or deed done specifically for the benefit of another. Jesus, our example, expressed His love throughout His earthly ministry for those He came to save. He went from village to village with His feet, He healed with His hands all who came to Him, He proclaimed the Gospel with His mouth, and yes, right up to His arrest in the Garden, He agonized in prayer upon His knees.

His love, referred to in the Greek as *agape*, is a sacrificial kind of love. It is a love that found its purest expression in Jesus laying down His life for the salvation of human-kind. Our expressions of His love for others, therefore, will always extract a personal cost from us as well. Like all forms of agape love, the price of loving others from our knees in prayer demands a sacrifice of our time, our effort, our comfort, and our personal preferences.

Such prayer, motivated by love, is what the Bible calls intercession. It can be said that intercession is agape love on its knees. It is a form of earnest prayer that is focused upon, and offered on behalf of, others. It is motivated by a selfless identification with the cares and concerns of others. An intercessor places him or herself in the shoes of another and, pleading for mercy, stands in the gap between them and God. An intercessor also takes a position as a hedge of protection, guarding from the attack of the enemy those for whom they are interceding (Ezekiel 22:29-30).

Throughout the Bible, the ground of authority from which intercession is made is rooted in one or more of three divine truths. It is based upon an appeal to the unchanging nature and character of God, His past merciful dealings with His creation, and/or the many promises of His coming kingdom and glory. Because the very idea of intercession originated in the heart of God, it is not something we can do in our own strength. On the contrary, it requires a humble dependence upon Him, a stirring by His Spirit of our heart of compassion, and a persistent faith to overcome every distraction and obstacle that would thwart our efforts.

Intercession is arguably the first and best thing we can do for someone. Consider this: intercession is presently the primary ministry of Jesus as He is seated in heavenly places at the right hand of the Father. The Bible clearly states that, since His resurrection and ascension, He "always lives to make intercession" (Hebrews 11:25 ESV). And here is the clincher, Paul the apostle tells us that we are seated with Him in the Spirit in that place of influence and authority and urged also like Christ, to "pray continually" (Ephesians 2:6; 1 Thessalonians 5:17).

Sadly, the ministry of intercession is often misunderstood and regarded as something only a select few are called and equipped to do. As a result, it is relegated in people's thinking to the super-spiritual, the prophetic types, the mission-minded, more women than men, or the shut-ins and elderly who have nothing better to do. This is an all too persistent misbelief! Recently, I was shocked to hear even a pastor excuse his own prayerlessness with the expressed assumption that intercession was something for the retirees to do because they had more time on their hands.

If, however, intercession is as we have established - a practical expression of Jesus' love for others - it is something everyone is expected to do, busy pastors included! It becomes the responsibility of every believer irregardless of calling, gifting, gender, or age. Everyone is called and gifted to love, none exempted. What better way to love someone than from our knees in intercession?

For further meditation and application:

Has gaining an understanding of intercession as an expression of love relieved you of any misconceptions or hesitancies you may have had about this form of prayer? How might you use love for others as a motivation to deepen your intercessory prayer life?

29

Praying a Hedge of Protection

And I sought for a man among them, that should make up
the hedge, and stand in the gap before me for the land, that I
should not destroy it: but I found none.
Ezekiel 22:30 KJV

One of the critical aspects of intercessory prayer is praying for a hedge of protection. The hedge, as a metaphor for spiritual protection, is used at least five times in the Bible to describe God's means of protecting both individuals and nations, Israel in particular. In each context it affords us a view beyond the veil that separates the natural from the spiritual world and gives us a glimpse into the spiritual warfare that is often required for the fulfillment of God's purposes.

Our first introduction to the hedge of protection is in the book of Job. Here we see Satan asking God for access to afflict Job. "Have you not put a hedge around him and his house and all that he has, on every side?" (Job 1:10 ESV) This hedge was obviously placed there by God to protect Job and was so effective that even Satan could not get at him. As the story unfolds, we see what can happen when God removes a hedge and how, even in doing so, He uses it to work good in Job's life by giving him a deeper revelation of Himself.

Next, we discover in the book of Isaiah how God prophesies of His intention to remove His hedge of protection from Israel, here likened to a vineyard, because of her waywardness. "And now I will tell you what I will do to my vineyard. I will remove its hedge, and it shall be devoured; I will break down its wall, and it shall be trampled down" (Isaiah 5:5 ESV). In this instance we again see God removing the hedge with the intention of ultimately turning Israel back to Him.

We find a nuance to this hedge metaphor in the book of Hosea. The prophet Hosea was married to a woman named Gomer who had a history of unfaithfulness. God purposely used her as an allegory for the nation of Israel and in the process lets Hosea and us in on a spiritual warfare secret. He says, "Therefore I will hedge up her way with thorns, and I will build a wall against her, so that she cannot find her paths. She shall pursue her lovers but not overtake them, and she shall seek them but shall not find them. Then she shall say, 'I will go and return to my first husband, for it was better for me then than now'" (Hosea 2:6-7 ESV).

To fully understand the import of what God is doing here, one must read the entire chapter, but, for the sake of brevity, I will summarize. The hedge of thorns that God places around Gomer effectively is used to separate her from all the evil influences in her life. It ultimately is meant to bring her to the end of herself, to her senses, and to a place of repentance before her husband and God.

You will notice that her confession to herself, "I will go and return . . . for it was better for me then and now," is basically the same confession the prodigal son made when he came to his senses in the familiar parable of Jesus. When the prodigal found himself with the pigs and was finally fed up with his wayward lifestyle, he confessed he had been better off in his father's house and determined, "I will set out and go back to my father" (Luke 15:18 NIV).

Can you see how praying for God to place a hedge of thorns around those who are wayward is a powerful intercession principle? This type of prayer can be used in interceding for both individuals and groups of people who are wandering from God, including prodigals, rebellious children, wayward spouses, and even the nations.

It must be said that this is not just a good idea or even something to be considered as an option. It is a necessity if we are going to be effective in interceding for God's purposes to be fulfilled in the lives of people we know and love.

God spoke sovereignly through the prophet Ezekiel on two separate occasions, pleading for intercessors who will step up and "make up a hedge." "Ye have not gone up into the gaps, neither made up the hedge for the house of Israel to stand in the battle in the day of the LORD" (Ezekiel 13:5 KJV). "And I sought for a man among them, that should make up the hedge, and stand in the gap before me for the land, that I should not destroy it: but I found none" (Ezekiel 22:30 KJV).

For further meditation and application:

Will you answer the call to step up and be a hedge builder from a place of prayer? Take a moment to consider if there is someone, or some situation, that could benefit from your praying a hedge of protection. Take some time right now, to pray that God would place a hedge about them, causing them to be kept from evil and return to Him, just as Gomer and the prodigal.

30

The Biblical Basis for Intercession

"Come now, and let us reason together," says the LORD.
Isaiah 1:18 NASB

Appealing to God to answer prayer can be likened to the ways in which children learn to convince their parents to act on their behalf. There are certain approaches that are more effective than others. In fact, the basis from which appeals are made can make a huge difference in how a request is answered.

When my firstborn son was three, he loved going to the park near our home where there was a playground. Like many parents, I was sometimes too preoccupied to give him the attention he desired and occasionally found myself procrastinating in doing the things I had promised him. One day, my little guy came up to me holding in his left hand a small bible we had given him. With his right hand he was pointing to it emphatically and looking me directly in the eyes as he pleaded "Go park!"

Since my conversion to Christianity in the year of his birth, I have always unashamedly made the Bible my handbook for life. My son knew that from seeing me studying it daily, searching its pages for guidance, using it for family devotions, and teaching from it as a pastor. Needless to say, his words and actions immediately melted my heart and, without hesitation, I put aside what I was doing in order to take him to the playground. Kids know how to touch their parents (and grandparents) hearts, don't they?

How much more can we, as children of our Heavenly Father, know how to touch His heart! The truth is there are proven ways to *convince* God to answer our prayers! I use the word "convince" here advisedly, understanding that prayer is not so much a process of convincing God as it is discovering His will and His ways in order to use that as the basis for our request.

A study of the great prayers of the Bible reveals that each of them drew upon foundational truths about God and His expectations of those who approach Him. The intercessors such as Abraham, Moses, Daniel, Esther, Nehemiah, Paul, and Jesus all presented their requests to God with what may be termed reasoned arguments. A closer examination reveals that their "reasoning" was based upon one or more of seven foundational Biblical principles.

These principles form the basis from which all effective intercession must be made. If you or I intend to get answers to our prayers by "convincing" God to grant us our requests, we must present our case within the purview of these principles.

Here, then, is the Biblical basis for effective intercession. God answers prayer based upon an appeal to . . .

1. **God's Character – who He is and His ways.** Abraham appealed to God as the righteous judge in bargaining back and forth with God over the plight of Sodom (Genesis 18:25-26). Nehemiah pleads with God for Israelites based on His covenant keeping and loving nature (Nehemiah 1:5). Appealing to the very nature and character of God is one of the most powerful prayers we can offer because He will not and cannot deny Himself.

2. **God's Past Mercy and Dealings – His acts.** God's merciful intervention in the past reveals His kind intention and purpose for the future. Moses sought the favor of God on behalf of Israel by reminding God of how He brought them out of Egypt "with great power and a mighty hand." Moses did so in appealing to Him to use that same power to complete what He had started, in this case, by bringing them into the promised land (Exodus 32:11). Nehemiah presents a similar case before God with regard to the restoration of Jerusalem (Nehemiah 1:10). Each intercessor here is simply asking God, based on His past merciful dealings, to continue to act consistently in the future.

3. **God's Reputation and Honor – concern for the Glory of God.** The glory of God is a frequent and preeminent theme in most Biblical prayers. Moses appealed to God to uphold His reputation and glory as does Daniel and David (Exodus 32:12; Daniel 9:15-19; Psalms 57:5, 11). Paul says it best: "For from Him and through Him and for Him are all things. To Him be the glory forever! Amen" (Romans 11:36 NIV).

4. **God's Promises – that He will fulfill what He has promised.** Since God is not a man that He should lie, and all

the promises of God find their "Yes" in Christ, there is no stronger appeal to God than prayers based upon His many Scriptural promises (Numbers 23:19; 2 Corinthians 1:20). Whenever we pray, "God you said . . . ," there is a confidence and authority in the Spirit that releases the power of God to accomplish what we ask. Faith literally comes into and energizes our prayers when we confess God's Word (Romans 10:17).

5. Our Identification with Those for Whom we are Praying. God's identification with His creation in sending His son Jesus to die for our redemption is the gold standard of intercessory identification. The heart of God is moved to action by all those who identify so fully with those for whom they pray that they themselves are willing to enter into their suffering. In their intercession for Israel, both Moses and Paul confessed their own willingness to suffer personal rejection by God if it would lead to the salvation of the Jews (Exodus 32:32; Romans 9:3). The old adage about walking a mile in another's shoes is empowering advice when it comes to interceding effectively for others.

6. Our Prayer Offered in Humility – There are many references in the Bible to God's ready response to those who approach Him with humility. In fact, He tells us that He dwells "with those whose spirits are contrite and humble" (Isaiah 57:15 NLT). That is why He promises to give grace to the humble and save those who are contrite in spirit (Psalm 34:18, James 4:6). Is it any wonder therefore, that, when Abraham persists in reasoning with God on behalf of Sodom, we see him acknowledging, "Since I have begun, let me speak further to my Lord, even though I am but dust and ashes" (Genesis 18:27 NLT).

7. Our Persistent Faith – The writer to the Hebrews tells us that it is through faith and patience that we inherit God's promises, and without faith it is impossible to please God (Hebrews 6:12, 11:6). Jesus, in His teachings on prayer, frequently emphasized persistent faith with such parables as the shameless audacity of the friend at midnight or the incessant persistence of the widow with the unjust judge (Luke 5:1-13; 18:1-6). Abraham's approach to God in prayer is a great example of this principle. He demonstrated a remarkable persistence in negotiating downward from the presence of 50 to 10 righteous people as reason for God to spare His judgment upon Sodom (Genesis 18:24-33).

When God says "Come now, and let us reason together," it is as though He is inviting us into the courtroom of heaven to present before Him a reasoned and convincing case as to why He should grant our request. The context of this verse is an invitation given by God to the prophet Isaiah to *reason* with Him in prayer in order to thwart the impending judgments coming upon Judah and Jerusalem.

As in any court room, there are proper ways in which to approach the bench and make requests. First it must be duly noted that only those who come in Jesus name, professing Jesus as their advocate, will be welcomed. These seven principles are tried and true ways in which the judge of all the earth has chosen to respond and act on behalf of those who come to Him. Basing our prayers on one or more of them provides us confidence in being heard and an assurance that an answer is forthcoming (1 John 5:15).

For further meditation and application:

Has your experience in intercession been consistent with these principles? Are there other ways or principles upon which God has led you to intercede?

31

Guidelines for Effective Intercession

A Step-by-Step Guide for Engaging in a
Time of Intercessory Prayer

Intercession is defined as praying for others as directed, energized, and empowered by the Holy Spirit. God's Word declares we are to make intercession for all men (1 Timothy 2:1). It is to "stand in the gap" between others and God, pleading on their behalf in the Spirit, and to "make up a hedge" against the enemy (Ezekiel 22:30; 13:5; Job 1:9-12).

My introduction to intercessory prayer, and the foundational principles for effective intercession, came through the teachings of Joy Dawson of Youth With A Mission (YWAM). God took Joy, in the 1970s, from being a simple New Zealand housewife schooled by the Spirit in the ways of personal intercession, and catapulted her on to the YWAM world stage. Since then, the depth of her experience and teaching on intercession has been used by God to raise up generations of intercessors.

The following ten principles are taken from Joy's teachings and are provided here as a step-by-step guide for engaging in a time of intercession. They are proven principles used for decades by countless thousands of intercessors and wannabe intercessors. They can be used by you as an individual or with a group of people.

1. **Make very sure your heart is clean before God, by giving the Holy Spirit time to convict, should there be any unconfessed sin.** The Bible warns "if I regard iniquity in my heart, the Lord will not hear me" (Psalm 66:18 KJV). Therefore it is helpful to pray like David, "search me, O God and know my heart, try me and know my thoughts; and see if there be any wicked way in me, and lead me in the way everlasting" (Psalm 139:23-24 ASV).

2. **Die to your own imaginations, desires, burdens, reasonings and preconceived ideas – for what you feel you should pray.** There are many Scriptures that encourage us to do this as a simple act of our will. "Gird up the loins of your mind" (1 Peter 1:13 KJV). "Casting down imaginations, and every high thing that exalts itself against the knowledge of God, and bringing into captivity every thought to the obedience of Christ" (2 Corinthians 10:5 KJV). When God says "my thoughts are not your thoughts" He is encouraging us to put aside our preconceived thoughts because, "he who trusts in his own mind is a fool" (Isaiah 55:8; Proverbs 28:26 ESV). Therefore "lean not on your own understanding" (Proverbs 3:5 ESV).

3. **Acknowledge you can't really pray without the direction and energy of the Holy Spirit.** Cling to and confess the great promises of the Holy Spirit's help when we

pray. "The Spirit also helps us in our weakness, for we do not know how to pray as we should" (Romans 8:26 NASB; Luke 24:49; Acts 1:8).

4. Ask God to completely control you by His Spirit. We desperately need to invite the presence of the Holy Spirit and ask Him to direct the intercession time. Jesus promised that "when he, the Spirit of truth, comes, he will guide you into all the truth. He will glorify me because it is from me that he will receive what he will make known to you." (John 16:13-14 NIV). In addition Jesus said "how much more will your heavenly Father give the Holy Spirit to those who ask Him?" (Luke 11:13 NLT) Therefore, take time to ask to "be filled with the Spirit" (Ephesian 5:18). **And then, thank Him for doing so,** for "without faith it is impossible to please God" (Hebrews 11:6 NIV).

5. Praise God now in faith for the remarkable prayer time you are going to have. He is a remarkable God and will do something consistent with His character. "Enter into His gates with thanksgiving and His courts with praise" (Psalm 100:4 NIV). "Praise Him for His mighty acts' praise Him according to His excellent greatness" (Psalm 150:2 ESV).

6. Deal aggressively with the enemy. Take authority given you as a child of God by Jesus Christ and command Satan and demon powers to be silent. Come against him in the all-powerful name of the Lord Jesus Christ and with the "sword of the Spirit" – the word of God (Ephesians 6:17). Jesus gave us this authority and it is imperative for us to use it! "Behold, I have given you authority to tread on serpents and scorpions, and over all the power of the enemy, and nothing shall hurt you" (Luke 10:19 ESV). For "greater is He that is in you, than he that is in the world" (1 John 4:4 KJV). Therefore "be sober, be vigilant; because your adversary, the devil, as a roaring lion walks about seeking whom he may devour; whom resist him steadfast in the faith" (1 Peter 5:8-9 AKJV). "Submit yourselves therefore to God. Resist the devil and he will flee from you. Draw near to God and He will draw near to you" (James 4:7-8 AKJV).

7. Ask for the fear of the Lord to speak out what He gives you and only what He gives you. Having a healthy fear of the Lord has its benefits. "In the fear of the Lord one has strong confidence" (Proverbs 14:26 ESV). "The fear of the Lord is the beginning of wisdom" (Proverbs 9:10 NIV). "The fear of the Lord is to hate evil" (Proverbs 8:13 NIV). Pray for boldness to step out and pray what you sense the Holy Spirit is putting on your heart. "Grant to your servants, that with all boldness they may speak your word" (Acts 4:30 AKJV). "The fear of man brings a snare" (Proverbs 29:25 NASB).

8. Wait in silent expectancy, giving God time to disclose all He would say to you regarding a particular burden. As you listen for the whisper of the Holy Spirit be sensitive to the ways in which He typically speaks to you – whether through a Scripture, a thought or impression, a word or phrase, perhaps even a vision. Then, in faith, speak out what God has brought to your mind, believing that "My sheep hear my voice . . . and they follow me" (John 10:27 ESV).

Believe Him to show you the subject(s) for which you should pray and then give you the understanding on how to pray for them. "Wisdom is the principle thing; therefore get wisdom: and with all your getting, get understanding" (Proverbs 4:7 AKJV).

9. Now pray out as the Spirit leads you (1 Corinthians 14:15, Jude 20, Ephesians 6:18). Be sure to pray all the prayers for one subject before proceeding to the next.

10. When God ceases to bring things to your mind to pray, finish by praising and thanking Him for what He has done, reminding yourself: "For from Him and through Him and for Him are all things," and that means the glory (Romans 11:36 NIV)!

Other Suggestions:
Always have your bible with you, should God want to give you directions or confirmation from it. "Your word is a lamp to my feet and a light to my path" (Psalm 119:105 ESV).

For further meditation and application:

Can you see how these steps can lead you into an engaging and effective time of intercession? At your earliest convenience, set aside 30-60 minutes to use these principles for a time of personal intercession. Also consider using them in a small group prayer meeting. Take time, after step eight, to have people share what they are sensing before entering into a time of prayer for the things for which the group is burdened.

32

Six Prayers God Always Answers

You do not have, because you do not ask God.
James 4:2 NIV

We find in the book of James one of the clearest, most succinct teachings on prayer contained anywhere in the Bible. In just six verses, James, the brother of Jesus and someone who should know something about prayer, encourages his readers with six different prayers that God loves to answer. The underlying reason for his emphasis on prayer in this epistle is stated in the words "you do not have, because you do not ask God." It should go without saying, but needs to be said again and again because we are so prone to forget: **we need to pray to get answers to prayer.** The answers we desire only come from prayers that are prayed. The more we pray, the more answers we get. It is that simple.

That having been said, here are the six prayers that always get answers from God. They are taken from the passage in James 5:13-18.

1. Hardship Prayers – "Are any of you suffering hardships? You should pray" (vs. 13a). For those suffering hardships, affliction, and troubles of any kind, we need to understand that God is "close to the brokenhearted" and promises to "rescue those whose spirits are crushed" (Psalm 34:18 NLT). He is a compassionate and merciful God who extends His steadfast love to those in need as faithfully as the rising of the sun each morning (Lamentations 3:32).

2. Praise Prayers – "Are any of you happy? You should sing praises" (vs. 13b). Praise to God is one of the most powerful prayers that can be prayed, not only in happy times, but also in times of trial. It is the language of heaven – where praise surrounds the Throne of God day and night. That is why we are told to enter His gates with thanksgiving and His courts with praise, and why the Lord's prayer begins with hallowing His name (Psalm 100:4; Matthew 6:9). God loves to release His power in response to praise just as He did when Jehoshaphat and his army went out to battle led by the worshippers (2 Chronicles 20). Praise not only ushers us into His presence and releases His power, but it also gives us His perspective as to how we should be praying.

3. Agreement Prayers – "Are any of you sick? You should call for the elders of the church to come and pray over you, anointing you with oil in the name of the Lord" (vs. 14). Jesus promised to be present wherever two or three are gathered in His name, saying "if two of you on earth agree about anything they ask for, it will be done for them by my Father in heaven" (Matthew 18:19-20). He said this to underscore for us the multiplied power of agreement in prayer. Just imagine: if one person can chase a thousand and two ten thousand, what can three or more do (Deuteronomy 32:30)?

4. Faith-Filled Prayers – "Such a prayer offered in faith will heal the sick, and the Lord will make you well" (vs.15a). When prayers are accompanied by faith, things kick into overdrive. Having unshakeable faith in God releases Christ's authority to the pray-er to command every mountain hindering an answer to one's prayer to be picked up and thrown into the sea (Mark 11:22-23). "Therefore I tell you, whatever you ask for in prayer, believe that you have received it, and it will be yours" (Mark 11:24). I will share more on this topic of faith and prayer in the next two chapters.

5. Repentance Prayers – "And if you have committed any sins, you will be forgiven. Confess your sins to each other and pray for each other so that you may be healed" (vs. 15b-16). One of the great promises in all the Bible is "if we confess our sins, God is faithful and just to forgive us our sins and cleanse us from all unrighteousness" (1 John 1:9). God will never not answer this prayer. To do so would deny His very nature and the reason He sent His son, Jesus, to die on the cross.

6. Persistent Prayers – "Elijah was as human as we are, and yet when he prayed earnestly that no rain would fall, none fell for three and a half years! Then, when he prayed again, the sky sent down rain and the earth began to yield its crops" (vs. 17-18). James uses a quintessential illustration of the power of persistent prayer taken from the life of Elijah (1 Kings 18). Even the great prophet had to pray multiple times, seven to be exact, before rain came. But he persisted, and God answered! Jesus said it best when He exhorted His disciples that "they should always pray and never give up" (Luke 18:1)!

For further meditation and application:

If you have been in a drought of unanswered prayer, identify one of these six prayers that best fits your present situation. Take some time right now to pray an appropriate prayer, based on these scriptural examples and God's faithfulness. Keep praying until you have confidence God is hearing your prayer.

33

Praying in the Spirit

Pray in the Spirit at all times and on every occasion.
Ephesians 6:18 NLT

Igniting and fueling an impassioned prayer life is only possible through an utter dependence upon the Holy Spirit. The Biblical phraseology for Spirit-dependent communication with God is *praying in the Spirit*. The Apostle Paul states it succinctly when he urges the Ephesians to "pray in the Spirit on *all* times and on *every* occasion" (Ephesians 6:18 NIV *emphasis added*). It is readily evident from this verse that praying in the Spirit is the ONLY acceptable way in which to pray. The use of the words "all" and "every" leaves no room for any other viable options. In short, prayer that is not Spirit bred, Spirit led, and Spirit fed, is really dead.

Understanding what it means to *pray in the Spirit* is therefore critical to developing and nurturing an impassioned prayer life. To pray in the Spirit has several applications. I would be the first to admit that I am not a theologian. As a lifelong student of the Bible I would describe myself as a Biblical practitioner, one who seeks to understand the Bible and practically apply it to my life. What I have to share therefore, about the various ways in which we can pray in the Spirit, is birthed out of that perspective.

First, being "in the Spirit" is a God-conscious frame of mind - whether during worship, in prayer, or even while serving God. It is a state of awareness of God's presence, dependence upon His power, and surrender to His will. Another way of understanding this is to think of it as being *tuned into* or *in tune with* the Spirit. To be *tuned into* the Holy Spirit conveys listening attentively to what He has to say. To be *in tune with* Him means to be in full accord or agreement.

Being *in the Spirit* is a result of a conscious decision to be sensitive to what the Holy Spirit is saying and doing. This ushers the pray-er into the presence of the Lord and it is in His presence where Spirit-led prayer is birthed. **Praying in the Spirit requires seeking His presence before asking for His presents.**

In practice, praying in the Spirit is simply allowing the Holy Spirit to pray *through* us. It can take place in several ways, depending on how we are moved by the Spirit to give utterance to our prayers. In times of utter weakness, when no words seem adequate to express the depths of our heart's wrestling's, the Holy Spirit sovereignly intervenes. He intercedes for us through our tears, sighs, and "groanings too deep for words" (Romans 8:26 ESV). As a rule, these "groanings" refer to wordless expressions of emotion as a person pours out their heart to God.

Closely akin to these unintelligible groanings, in which the Holy Spirit prays directly through us, is a form of prayer known as praying in tongues. In this instance, the Holy Spirit enables us to speak directly to God in an unlearned language - described in the Bible as an unknown tongue and uttering mysteries in the Spirit (1 Corinthians 14:2; 13-15). It is one of the gifts of the Holy Spirit listed in 1 Corinthians 12, which the Spirit distributes as He determines (vs. 10-11). Its value, both for building up a person's faith and praying with fervor when no intelligible words come, is lauded by the Apostle Paul, who himself claimed to speak in tongues more than anyone (1 Corinthians 14:4-5; 18). Using the gift of tongues is a very empowering way to pray. It releases faith in knowing that you are not limited by your comprehension, but that the Spirit is praying according to the will of God for things only He can know (1 John 5:14-15).

It is both comforting and empowering to know that God helps us by His Spirit when we do not know how to pray. The wonder of it all is the Holy Spirit knows how we ought to pray, and chooses to pray in our stead while by-passing our intellectual understanding.

The most common way, however, that people *pray in the Spirit* is by petitioning God with intelligible words in their native language. The Holy Spirit has a myriad of ways in which to inspire and guide a person who is *in the Spirit* and praying. He will typically move upon a person's heart by giving them an impression or a burden, a revelation or an insight, a picture or a vision, a word or a phrase. That understanding begins to so grip them that they become faith inspired to speak forth in prayer what they are sensing and seeing.

Being responsive in faith to the Holy Spirit's whispers and nudges, is the key to praying in the Spirit. Faith and praying in the Spirit go hand in hand. Jude underscores this in his epistle. "But you, beloved, building yourselves up in your most holy faith and praying in the Holy Spirit" (Jude 1:20 ESV). Prayers that are a response to the promptings of the Holy Spirit, and breathed in faith, will open the windows of heaven, unlock any door on earth, and rattle the gates of hell.

We must continually thank God for the gift of the Holy Spirit to help us in our praying, always keeping in mind that it is "Not by might nor by power, but by my Spirit,' says the LORD Almighty" (Zechariah 4:6 NIV).

For further meditation and application:

Think of a time when you knew you were "praying in the Spirit." How did you know? Did you feel faith rising as you prayed? What was the result of your prayer - for yourself and for the person or thing for which you prayed? Did it change the way you prayed for that same concern the next time? If so, how?

34

The Prayer of Faith

And the prayer of faith shall deliver the sick, and the Lord shall raise him up. . . Confess your faults one to another, and pray one for another, that you may be healed. The effectual fervent prayer of a righteous man avails much.
James 5:15-16 KJV 2000

James refers here to a specific type of prayer he terms the "prayer of faith." In verse sixteen he gives us a primer on prayer that may be one of the best explanations of effective praying in the entire Bible. Specifically, in this one verse he provides insight into the three primary ingredients for praying a prayer of faith

James, the author of this book by the same name, is uniquely qualified to do so because, as most scholars agree, he was the brother of the Lord Jesus Christ and the lead elder in the early Jerusalem church (Matthew 13:55; Acts 15:13). He was also highly esteemed by the two leading apostles of the day, Peter and Paul (Acts 12:17; Galatians 2:9). If anyone had firsthand knowledge about the prayer of faith, it was James.

Bottom line, the measure of an effective prayer is ultimately whether or not it gets an answer. What would be the point of asking someone for something if there was no expectation or hope of getting an affirmative reply? That is where faith comes in. Prayer, by its very nature, is undertaken from a place of faith, trusting that there is a God who is greater than us and who hears and answers our requests. Prayer is a faith proposition from beginning to end. "And without faith it is impossible to please God, because anyone who comes to Him must believe that He exists and that He rewards those who earnestly seek Him" (Hebrews 11:6 NIV).

Prayer is based on a trust in someone who is not seen, who initiates something from a realm that is unseen, and who causes it to make its appearance in a realm that is seen. Faith, then, truly is fixing "our eyes not on what is seen, but on what is unseen . . . but what is unseen is eternal" (2 Corinthians 4:18 NIV). James is underscoring this when he writes "the effectual fervent prayer of a righteous man avails much" (vs. 16b).

There are three defining characteristics of the prayer of faith in this verse, and they specify that it must be:

1. PURE HEARTED – Faith in God hearing us is rooted in two things. First, it requires having a heart that is pure in righteousness because it has been cleansed by the blood of Jesus through repentance and forgiveness of sins. James makes this clear in these verses as he encourages "confess your faults one to another and pray for one another, that you may be healed" (James 5:16 KJV 2000).

Secondly, it requires having a heart that is pure in its motives because a person's will has been fully yielded to the will of God. The Greek word from which the phrase "righteous man" is translated is *dikaios* which specifically refers to a righteous person who is just or impartial. **It is a term that conveys a righteousness both in spirit and in motive.** It is a noun that could be used to describe a judge who is unbiased or unprejudiced in making a ruling on a case. Whenever a person prays from a place of having fully relinquished their own desires, that prayer is a prayer they can be confident God will answer.

2. PASSION FUELED – James tells us that the prayer of faith is "fervent." He describes this type of prayer using a Greek word *energeo* from which we get our English words energy and energized. *Energeo*, depending on the English version of this verse, is translated as "effectual fervent" prayer and means to be fully engaged in, to be mighty in, or working at. It conveys a passionate, no-holds-barred level of commitment to prayer. Working to move a big obstacle and overcome inertia requires a steady, all-out effort and determination to persist no matter what the cost.

Passion summons answers to prayer like nothing else. James illustrates this in the next two verses when he cites Elijah's faith fueled by his earnest persistence in praying for both Israel's drought and its eventual relief (vs. 17-18). A common phrase, used over twenty-six times in the Bible, for this passion-fueled type of prayer is "crying unto the Lord." Jacob wrestled with the angel all night, begging, "I will not let you go unless you bless me" (Genesis 32:26). Jesus himself "offered up prayers and petitions with loud cries and tears to the one who could save Him from death, and

He was heard because of His reverent submission" (Hebrews 5:7 NIV).

3. PROMISE BASED – James says the prayer of faith "avails much." The Greek verb which he chooses here is *ischuo* meaning to have power, to be of strength, and to prevail. Availing and prevailing prayers are always based on the Word of God. **Another way of saying this is that God's Word is what makes prayer work.** That is the secret to the prayer of faith. Relying upon and confessing the Word of God releases faith (Romans 10:17). This is often referred to as *praying the promises*. Everything around us may be trembling and falling, but, as long as we stand upon and pray God's Word, we will prevail. When promises from Scripture proceed from our mouths in prayer they do not return void but will accomplish that for which they were sent (Isaiah 55:11).

Just like the saints of old, present day saints continue to see the prayer of faith move the heart and hand of God like nothing else. Their testimonies are a compelling invitation for us to pray in a similar manner. To summarize, the three ingredients of the prayer of faith **are** a pure heart made righteous by faith, a passion-fueled commitment to persist, and a promise-based prayer.

For further meditation and application:

Can you think of a time, in your communion with God, when you have prayed the prayer of faith? Was your experience similar to James' description of the prayer of faith? How? How was it dissimilar? What can you learn from all of this which will help you pray more effectively in the future?

35

Praying Through

Pray Until Something Happens!

Praying for something with persistence is often a challenge. Putting the time in is one thing, but being earnestly engaged and getting into a place of praying effectively is quite another. To do so requires battling through lethargy, distractions, rote babblings, and just plain old unbelief and doubt.

The truth is that to be effective in prayer one must be committed to doing what the saints of old called "praying through." In essence, praying through means praying until something happens. **You might call it the PUSH method of praying** – Pray Until Something Happens.

That "something" does not have to be the actual answer to the prayer, and in most cases it is not. But that "something" is invariably the assurance that you have been heard. That assurance is the evidence that you have prayed yourself into to a place of faith (Hebrews 11:6). There is a release in one's spirit that comes when you know that God has heard because we know that when He hears us, an answer is on the way (1 John 5:15).

Isaiah likens earnest prayer and intercession to the travail of labor in giving birth (Isaiah 66:7-8). Praying through is like that. It is hard work, and it requires an engagement of one's entire being in bringing forth the desired result. While there are many different ways to pray, praying through is not a quiet, contemplative, sweet lullaby, by-and-by type of praying. It is most often a forceful, loud, emotion-filled, physically taxing, heart-wrenching type of praying. Advancing the kingdom of God often requires such "forceful" prayer. Jesus' reference to this literally means to "eagerly claim for oneself" (Matthew 11:12).

Here are some examples of individuals who knew how to pray through.
- **Jesus** – "During the days of Jesus' life on earth, he offered up prayers and petitions *with loud cries and tears* to the one who could save him from death, and he was heard because of his reverent submission" (Hebrews 5:7 NIV *emphasis added*).
- **Jacob** – "He struggled with the angel and overcame him; *he wept and begged* for his favor" (Hosea 12:4 NIV *emphasis added*).
- **Hannah** – "Hannah was in *deep anguish, crying bitterly* as she prayed to the LORD" (1 Samuel 1:10 NLT *emphasis added*). Her prayer that the Lord would give her a child was so demonstrative that Eli the priest thought she was drunk.
- **Elijah** – "*Prayed fervently*" (James 5:17 *emphasis added*). **He prayed seven times** that it would rain, "*bowed low* to

the ground and prayed with *his face between his knees"* (1 Kings 18:42-46 NLT *emphasis added*).

- **Hezekiah** - "Hezekiah received the letter from the messengers and read it. Then he went up to the temple of the LORD and *spread it out before the LORD"* (Isaiah 37:14 NIV *emphasis added*). What Hezekiah did here, when threatened by King Sennacharib of Assyria, was literally lay it all out before the Lord. In so doing, he cast his burden fully on the Lord (Psalm 55:22).

Do you see the picture of *praying through* **that emerges here?** Praying through is often marked by loud cries and tears, anguished outbursts, persistent repetition, and bowing low to the ground. As a result, at times I have found I need to move my place of prayer from my study to the basement so I can let it rip. If we prayed more like that, we just might get the same results they did.

For further meditation and application:

Are you carrying a burden for which you have prayed, but still lack the assurance that God has heard you? If so, God may be prompting you to apply the PUSH method to your praying. You'll know you have prayed through when you take the time to *Pray Until Something Happens.*

36

Power in the Name of Jesus

If you ask me anything in my name, I will do it.
John 14:14 ESV

Some of the most impactful mission trips that I have taken have been into a remote village named God's River (Manto Sipi) in Northern Manitoba. It is one of a number of Cree Nation settlements dotting that vast expanse of lakes and forest accessible only by air or winter ice roads. In the 1960's and 1970's there were a couple of pioneering ministers from Minnesota who ventured into that country to serve those communities and bring the Gospel.

I was enriched and blessed to partner with one of those men, Jesse Graham. His first foray into God's River was somewhat unusual. He did not know anyone when he stepped off the small twin engine plane onto the gravel airstrip, coming only at the invitation of the Holy Spirit. All he had with him was his Bible, a small duffel bag, and his guitar. From that inauspicious beginning, he established a fledgling indigenous church with one of his new converts as the pastor. Jesse made annual trips into the village, and on a number of occasions, at his invitation, I joined him to participate in God's work in God's River.

Another of those missionary pioneers was a man named Maynard Howe. Maynard became a kind of legend in the north by establishing churches in many of the Cree villages. Countless remarkable testimonies of salvation among the Cree people came out of the pioneering work by these men.

One testimony that made an indelible impression upon me was a story related by Maynard of a native man who had been a medicine man in one of the villages. He had become very sick and, by his own account, had died. In death, as he was descending into utter darkness on his way to hell, he began to cry out to all his spirits whom he had served. There was no response. No matter how fervently he prayed and cried out to these various gods nothing happened nor could they stop his free fall into the abyss. Finally, in sheer desperation, out of the recesses of a memory of a gospel message heard years earlier, he blurted out the name of Jesus. Instantly, like being grasped from above, he was pulled out of that dark pit and felt himself being drawn upward to a bright light.

When he awoke, he asked those attending him at his deathbed, "Tell me about Jesus, I want to know this man that just saved me." Nobody around him could answer his questions. When he was fully healed, he eventually found Maynard and accepted Jesus Christ as his Savior.

I love this story because it illustrates so clearly two fundamental truths about the power that resides in the name of Jesus. First, with regards to salvation we see, that indeed "there is salvation in no one else, for there is no other name under heaven given among men by which we must be saved" (Acts 4:12 ESV). That was literally the case for the medicine man who found that only the name of Jesus could save him from the pit of darkness and hell.

Secondly, and this is of the utmost importance to bear in mind when it comes to seeing our prayers answered, we must pray in the name of Jesus! The salient stipulation and preeminent promise associated with answered prayer in Jesus' teaching is summed up in this one verse. "If you ask anything in my name, I will do it" (John 14:14 NIV). Jesus said this exact same thing four times to underscore it (John 14:13; 15:14; 16:23). The medicine man's prayer only found an answer in uttering the name of Jesus.

To ask for something in Jesus' name requires more than simply mouthing the words. The critical thing is to do it in the nature of Jesus because, for Him, name and nature are synonymous. To ask in His name means to ask in His nature. To ask in His nature means submitting ourselves to, and aligning ourselves with, His nature or character under His lordship. Therein lies the power "so that whatever you ask in my name the Father will give you" (John 15:16 NIV).

For further meditation and application:

Take a few moments now to reflect upon your use of the name of Jesus in your praying. Has reading this chapter given you a greater sense of the imperative of praying in the name of Jesus? If so, what kind of commitment are you willing to make to be sure that your prayers are in accordance with His promises to answer those who ask in His name?

37

The Most Powerful Prayer
You Can Pray!

*Give thanks in all circumstances, for this is
God's will for you in Christ Jesus.*
1 Thessalonians 5:18 NIV

Some circumstances make it difficult for us to know how to pray. There is a prayer that anyone, anywhere, at any time can pray and be confident that God has heard and will answer.

Like most prayer, the words are not as important as the attitude of heart that expresses it.

Whenever **Jesus** prayed it, God the Father worked miracles (Mark 6:41).

The apostle **Paul** said that whenever you pray, you should always pray this. More than twenty times in the New Testament, Paul himself prayed this prayer or encouraged others to do so (Philippians 4:6; 1 Thessalonians 5:13).

In the Old Testament, **David**, Israel's greatest king and psalmist, prayed this prayer more than twenty-five times as well. You'll find most of those prayers in the Psalms. David encouraged us that it was the key to entering God's Presence (Psalm 100:1).

Great battles were won when people prayed this prayer. One of the best examples is the account of **King Jehoshaphat** and the people of Judah using this prayer as they entered into battle against the attacking Moabites and Ammonites (2 Chronicles 20:21).

It is the SIMPLEST and SHORTEST PRAYER in the Bible. You don't need to memorize it. It is probably the GREATEST PRAYER of FAITH a person can pray. Yet, although this prayer is encouraged throughout the Bible and is so powerful, **MOST PEOPLE typically FORGET to pray this prayer.**

In fact, Jesus' encounter with one group of people indicates that perhaps **ONLY ONE IN TEN PRAY IT**. Plus He greatly commended those who did (Luke 17:16-17).

What is this prayer? Simply saying "thanks" to God! Paul writes "Give thanks in all circumstances, for this is God's will for you in Christ Jesus" (1 Thessalonians 5:18 NIV).

For further meditation and application:

Pause right now and pray some prayers of "thanks" to God. Thank Him for the good things that have happened in your life. And this is important, thank Him for the bad things as well. In giving thanks for the difficult things, like the saints of old, you are praying the most powerful prayer you can pray. Like them, expect similar results!

38

Why Prayer is Not an Option

As long as Moses held up his hands, the Israelites were winning, but whenever he lowered his hands, the Amalekites were winning. Exodus 17:11 NIV

Some things only happen if someone prays and will not happen if someone does not pray. That is the intriguing message from this verse. If that is true, it is the most compelling reason there is for a person to pray – especially for the things we want to happen.

This startling lesson on prayer took place shortly after the children of Israel left Egypt and began their journey into the wilderness toward the promised land. They were attacked by a people called the Amalekites, and Moses sent Joshua out with an army of men to fight them. Moses, along with his brother Aaron and another leader by the name of Hur, went up on a nearby hill to watch and pray.

Unlike so many of us, they had the enviable benefit of observing exactly what happened when they prayed and when they didn't. It was like God Himself had engineered

a lab experiment on prayer. Having the vantage point of watching from the top of a hill, they were able to see the direct results of their prayers as they surveyed the battle raging in the valley below.

It did not take long for them to discover that winning the battle was directly dependent upon their prayers. The problem was they had to figure out a way to enable Moses to keep from dropping his hands in prayer. So they "took a stone and put it under him and he sat on it. Aaron and Hur held his hands up--one on one side, one on the other--so that his hands remained steady till sunset" (vs. 12). That clearly did the trick, and we are told "So Joshua overcame the Amalekite army with the sword" (vs. 13).

This lesson on the priority of prayer was so important that God instructed Moses to record the details of the victory on a scroll so that it would never be forgotten (vs. 14). Moses himself was so overwhelmed by the significance of this revelation about prayer that he "built an altar and called it The Lord is my Banner" (vs. 15). "He said, 'For hands were lifted up to the throne of the Lord'" (vs. 16). He did not ever want to forget about the deciding difference prayer makes.

I think we can now surmise from this passage of scripture in Exodus 18 that the message is loud and clear: **some things only happen if someone prays and will not happen if someone does not pray.** However the way God answers prayer, His will and His timing are so cloaked in mystery that we do not know what things in life specifically fall under this rule. That is always the x factor when it comes to prayer. It therefore challenges us to take seriously the admonition to "pray without ceasing" - especially for the things we want to happen (1 Thessalonians 5:17).

Based on this principle of prayer we can see why Augustine of Hippo said: "Pray as if everything depends on God. Work as if everything depends upon you." That is what Israel through Moses and Joshua did, and God gave them an amazing victory. Should the desired victories in yours and my life be won with any less effort?

For further meditation and application:

Is there some challenge in your life, that for whatever reason, you have neglected to bring to the Lord in prayer? If so, let me encourage you to use it as a kind of "lab experiment" on prayer. Write down the date and a simple prayer for victory in this challenge. Resolve to pray this prayer frequently and note the results. Like Moses, you may be surprised at the difference your prayers make!

39

Assumptions - The Biggest Enemies of Prayer

Once more the Philistines raided the valley; so David inquired of God again, and God answered him.
1 Chronicles 14:13-14 NIV

The biggest enemy of prayer is assumptions. Now, I am talking here about false assumptions. Assumptions lead to presumption and presumption preempts prayer. The biggest false assumption of them all is that you do not need to pray because God will take care of it or do it anyway. When we assume that, we are basically saying that prayer does not make a difference. That, of course, is a foolhardy and dangerous position to take.

But the entire Bible tells us just the opposite. As John Wesley put it so succinctly: "God does nothing except in answer to prayer." Everything God says about prayer and the way His people relate to Him in the Scriptures through prayer confirm this fact. Repeatedly, He tells us that we are to seek Him so that He can act on our behalf. Jesus summed it all up when He told us to ask, seek and knock (Luke 11:9-10). From God's dealings with Abraham, Moses and the children of Israel, King David and the kings, to the prophets and leaders of the restoration, we see prayer as the central means of moving His hand and establishing His will in the earth (Genesis 18; Exodus 17:8-13; 1 Chronicles 14:8-17; Nehemiah 1).

One of the most inspirational accounts of no-presumption prayer is the story of David fending off two identical, back-to-back attacks by the Philistines (1 Chronicles 14:8-17). It illustrates how refraining from presumption motivates a person to pray. In response to the first attack, David prayed and asked God whether or not he should go to battle against them and if he would win. God gave the go ahead; he attacked the Philistines and was victorious. But then they attacked again.

Based on his previous victory, David could easily have assumed that God would do the same thing again for him, and prayer was not necessary. Wisely however, he did not assume that. Once again he inquired of God, and this time he was given different instructions. God told him to circle around behind them and wait for this sign to commence the attack: the "sound of marching in the tops of the balsam trees" (vs. 14). David did as God commanded him and gained another victory.

I have also learned a few things from my own personal experience about the dangers of making false assumptions that lead to prayerlessness. **In addition to the root assumption that God will simply take care of things**

without prayer, here are six more assumptions that are enemies of prayer. Don't fall prey to them!

1. Don't assume God doesn't love or care for you. This is a huge hindrance to prayer. Unanswered prayer, misfortune, and/or sin in our lives all try to convince us that God will not be there for us this time. That is a lie. Nothing can separate you from the love of God which is in Christ Jesus (Romans 8:38-39). God is merciful and full of compassion. As that great old hymn reminds us "His eye is on the sparrow and He watches over you" (Matthew 10:29).

2. Don't assume God is not interested or it is too small a thing! If He has even the hairs of your head numbered, nothing you are concerned about is too insignificant for Him (Luke 12:7).

3. Don't assume it is too big a thing to bother praying about! Huge problems, insurmountable odds, and catastrophic events on a national or world scale can be overwhelming. But God invites us to pray because "the effectual, fervent prayer of a righteous man [or woman] availeth much" (James 5:16 KJV). Our seemingly insignificant prayer may not change the world but it can change one person's world.

4. Don't assume you can handle it yourself! "Trust in the Lord with all your heart and do not lean on your own understanding . . ." (Proverbs 3:5-6 NIV).

5. Don't assume your ideas and opinions are God's. We dare not assume that we know what God is thinking without asking Him. "His thoughts are not our thoughts" (Isaiah 55:8).

6. Don't assume God is on your side! This is a subtle temptation when we get into a relationship conflict. Like Joshua, we need to be reminded that God does not choose sides, but, rather, we must seek to align ourselves with Him and His will (Joshua 5:13-15).

For further meditation and application:
Do you have any assumptions to add to the list? What passage(s) of Scripture can you think of or find to counter that lie?

40

Never Forget
Prayer Makes a Difference

"Never stop praying." 1 Thessalonians 5:17 NLT

Never underestimate the difference a prayer can make. "Never stop praying" is one of the shortest verses in the Bible and yet it conveys a remarkable and unmistakable truth. Prayer makes a difference! Even when it may seem like a brief formality or something done simply out of habit, prayer is nonetheless important. I learned this in an unforgettably humorous way, back when I was a youth pastor.

One practice of prayer, since my early days as a believer, has been to pause before embarking on any long journey and ask God for His traveling mercies. Typically it is a spontaneous type of prayer asking for His presence and protection as I and those with me travel to our destination. It is as simple as bowing for a few moments while sitting in our vehicle just before starting out. As a leader I have always been particularly cognizant of the necessity of doing this whenever I have had a vehicle loaded with people ready to depart on an outing together.

One winter I chartered a school bus to take the youth from our church located in the Twin Cities (Minnesota) up into the woods of Northern Wisconsin for a weekend retreat. The retreat center was a rustic one that was situated just off an isolated forest road in the middle of nowhere. The scenery was spectacular. The bows of the tall pine trees were laden with snow and the white expanse of the nearby frozen lake provided a crystal clear contrast to the cloudless azure sky. All the students and counselors had a wonderful time participating in outdoor snow activities and then in the evening gathered around the fireplace for times together of worship and Bible teaching. It was the perfect retreat every youth pastor dreams of - no need to threaten sending someone home or to discipline some pranksters disrupting our sleep in the night.

Sunday afternoon, after the typical cajoling and herding, we finally had everyone on the bus and were ready to go. It had been a hectic time cleaning and packing up and we were an hour or so behind schedule with a four hour drive yet ahead of us. As I was standing at the head of the bus's aisle, having completed the head count, I was anxious to get rolling. The bus driver had closed the doors and was paused waiting to hit the road. I thought to myself "Now it's time to pray." But I can remember very clearly reasoning within myself "Oh it's really not all that important, it's just a formality anyway, we need to get on our way." And with that conversation in my head completed, I dropped the idea of prayer and gave the bus driver the nod to go.

The driver drove down the driveway and took a right onto the road. But for some reason his turn was too wide and our bus began plowing into the huge show banks lining the far side of the road. When we finally came to a stop, we were snowbound helplessly and precipitously at a nearly 45 degree angle straddling the shoulder and the ditch. Fearing that the bus would tip over, we had everyone get out as soon as possible. As all of us were standing on that desolate road we began wondering where to get help. Being miles from the nearest town, it could take hours before a tow truck would be able to find its way to us.

It was then that the deep conviction of the Holy Spirit came upon me. I realized that we were in the ditch because I had passed on a prompting to pray and underestimated the difference that prayer really makes. Having no other recourse, I shared with the entire group what I had done and asked their forgiveness. Then all of us prayed acknowledging to God that prayer does matter and asking Him to help us. No sooner had we finished saying "Amen" then we all had to clear the road because a vehicle was approaching. It pulled to a stop beside us and to our surprise it was a big Budweiser truck. The driver was a very congenial man and as he marveled at our predicament, he offered, "Why don't I try to pull you out?" He proceeded to drag out a huge chain and literally within minutes he had us towed back up onto the road. With profuse thanksgivings on our part, he was soon on his way and so were we.

Imagine, in a delay of a mere fifteen minutes, God had engineered an invaluable and indelible lesson about prayer that would impact me and many others for a lifetime: Never underestimate the power of your prayer! And here is

God's sense of humor, in the midst of our dilemma it is as if He was saying to us . . ."This Bud's for you!"

For further meditation and application:

Can you think of a time when you too readily dismissed the importance of praying for something? Do you have any stories of how God taught you the great value of prayer?

41

Waiting on the Lord

Wait on the LORD: be of good courage, and he shall
strengthen thine heart: wait, I say, on the LORD.
Psalm 27:14 KJV

One of the most challenging and perplexing aspects of
prayer is the period of time between the request and the
answer. That phase is commonly referred to as *waiting on the*
Lord. When prayers are answered quickly, the waiting
period is brief and buoyed by an expectant satisfaction and
relief in having made the request. But when the answer
lingers and the waiting period begins to slowly drag on,
waves of doubt and impatience gather strength as they
buffet the heart of the pray-er. It could be said that **waiting**
on the Lord is the test between the request and God's best.

This critical time of waiting on the Lord is often
characterized by confusion and weariness. Yet it is in this
waiting process, which God purposely allows, that prayer
does its deepest, most beneficial work in the heart of the
pray-er. As much as we would like to avoid it, it is the

necessary path God provides to purify our desires and prepare us to move from promise to provision.

It is understandable, therefore, that there are many scriptures extolling the virtues of waiting on the Lord. Waiting on the Lord and hoping in the Lord are frequently linked and sometimes even used interchangeably. "We wait in hope for the Lord," the psalmist tells us, "he is our help and our shield" (Psalm 33:20 NIV). "Praise awaits you, our God" (Psalm 65:1 NIV). And "I wait for the LORD, my whole being waits, and in his word I put my hope" (Psalm 130:5 NIV).

In the waiting process, hope in God's character and His word is like the oxygen that keeps us breathing words of praise while we wait for God to answer. We can see, therefore, how critical it is, in waiting for God to answer our prayers, to maintain a lifeline of hope by reminding ourselves of God's past faithfulness and many promises.

Waiting on the Lord is also frequently associated with building spiritual strength and courage. It might be likened to a free membership at a spiritual health club. To derive benefit, one must take advantage of all the training and equipment available there to build spiritual muscle and endurance. For example, consider the following exhortation. "Wait for the LORD; *be strong, and let your heart take courage*; wait for the LORD" (Psalm 27:14 NIV *emphasis added*). And take note of this prescriptive guarantee: "they who wait for *the LORD shall renew their strength*; they shall mount up with wings like eagles; they shall run and not be weary; they shall walk and not faint" (Isaiah 40:31 ESV *emphasis added*). What a promise! "Physical training is good, but training for godliness [by waiting on the Lord] is much better, promising benefits in this life and in the life to come" (1 Timothy 4:8 NLT).

Waiting on the Lord, however, is costly to our flesh. It is the price we pay for God's glory to be revealed in and through our lives. It is death to self on the installment plan. With each passing day, we must be willing to die to *our* demands and *our* timetables. For the most part, there are no easy ways out or quick fixes. Such expectations are more characteristic of the world's ways than God's ways. God's expectations and timetables are higher than man's. His concern is more for the inner work of the heart than the outworking of our circumstances.

Waiting exercises our heart to seek Him more earnestly and depend upon Him more desperately. It drives us to our knees and to depths of prayer and to an intimacy of relationship with God hitherto unexperienced. Sun-kissed days and fair blue skies do not extract heart felt cries directed toward heaven like storm-driven days and dark cloudy skies.

Waiting transforms us by purifying our motives and desires to align us with God's will for our lives. Like the refining of gold by fire, waiting on the Lord has a way of burning away the dross of fleshly ambition. It transforms us from babes demanding our own way to mature sons and daughters crying out for God's way. **It is a primary means that God uses to conform us to the image of His Son.** Like the request of the returning prodigal, our appeal to the Father changes from "give me" to "make me" (Luke 15:12, 19).

Consequently, waiting on the Lord is meant to strategically position us to be the kind of people upon whom God can freely pour forth His blessings. Our job is not to figure it all out, provide for ourselves, or twist God's arm. Nor dare we throw up our hands, do nothing, and abandon our hope that an answer will come.

In the next chapter I will share some practical things we can and should do while we are waiting on the Lord in order to maximize its benefits.

For further meditation and application:

Can you identify one or two major prayer requests that you have been waiting a long time for God's answer? What might God be doing in your life through this waiting process from which you can derive some spiritual benefit?

42

What to Do While You are
Waiting for an Answer

*I wait for the LORD, my whole being wait
and in his word I put my hope.*
Psalm 130:5 NIV

One of the perplexing aspects of prayer is not knowing
what to do in the period between the ask and the answer.
That phase, commonly referred to as *waiting on the Lord*,
is critical to an effective prayer life because it is often
where the battle for an answer is either won or lost. We all
have a tendency, when an answer is delayed, to be tempted
with casting away our confidence, giving up hope, and
letting our prayer wane.

Practically, what then should a person do while waiting on
the Lord to be enabled not only to hang in there but also,
hopefully, move the process along and maximize the
inherent benefits of such a time?

Here is some tried and tested wisdom from the teachings of Jesus and the Apostle Paul that is guaranteed to resuscitate a prayer that is gasping for hope.

1. KEEP PRAYING - Jesus emphasized to His disciples through the parable of the widow and the unjust judge that we "should always pray and not give up" (Luke 18:1 NIV). There are many stories in the Bible of men and women who persevered in prayer despite prolonged periods of heavenly silence and yet prevailed due to their persistence (e.g. Hannah, Elijah & Hebrews 11). Sometimes, however, we simply are at a loss for words. Having prayed for something for so long our energy and faith can become depleted. What then?

How do we stoke the dying flame of prayer while trusting the Holy Spirit to blow upon the embers?

First, we can ask others to pray for us. Enlisting the help of others to pray for us taps into a level of faith that can make up for our lack. One of the liabilities of prolonged prayer is a battle-weary faith. Reinforcements coming fresh to the front lines always bring with them invigorating faith and hope. All of us at times are like Moses and need an Aaron and a Hur to hold up our drooping arms as we persist in prayer (Exodus 17:12). The added benefit is the potential to release the power of the prayer of agreement when two or more agree (Matthew 18:19). It's like one chasing a thousand, but two putting ten thousand to flight (Deuteronomy 32:30).

Another big help is using crafted prayers. A secret to sustaining persistent prayer for something is to write out, or craft, a prayer based on scriptural promises that are meaningful to you and relevant to your situation. It is not unusual to become so dispirited after praying for something for a long time that one no longer has even enough energy to form the words in one's mouth to pray. At such times, a well-crafted prayer, as it is read, has the power to ignite faith and fire the imagination once again to believe God for a breakthrough.

Third, pray for the needs of others. When we intentionally focus our attention on praying for the needs of others, it helps to divert the emphasis off ourselves and our problems. Also, praying for others is like giving: the sowing and reaping principle sets in and releases an added measure of God's blessing in return upon our lives. Parenthetically, I have found that expanding my prayer purview to include such prayer burdens as our government, the nations, Israel, the persecuted church, and so on, renews my stamina in praying for my own needs.

2. KEEP PRAISING – It might be said that one of the most powerful prayers we can pray is in giving praise and thanks to God for unanswered prayer. That, in essence, is what Paul writes when he says, ". . . in everything give thanks; for this is God's will for you in Christ Jesus" (1 Thessalonians 5:18 NASB). There is power in praise. Praise leads us into God's *presence,* and in His presence we gain His *perspective,* and His perspective releases His *power* (Psalm 100; 149; 2 Chronicles 20). The psalmist David, who knew tons about waiting on the Lord, wrote, "Praise waits for you, O God in Zion" (Psalm 65:1 KJV 2000). So it might be said that praise invites God into our waiting time. A wonderful by product is that it renews our strength to continue waiting without fainting (Isaiah 40:31).

3. **KEEP PRESSING ON to Know the Lord** – God's ultimate purpose in the prayer process is to reveal Himself in an intimate relationship in which He makes us more Christ-like and centers our lives in His will to accomplish His purposes. In Philippians 3:10-14, written by the Apostle Paul, we find one of the most powerful crafted prayers ever written. In it Paul puts knowing Christ as the preeminent, overarching purpose of life. His prayer commitment to press on to "take hold of that for which Christ Jesus took hold of" him and to press on "toward the goal to win the prize" provides us a critical example of the real intention behind every prayer we pray (vs. 12; 14 NIV).

The abiding joy of the waiting process is experienced when, like Abraham, we discover the most fulfilling answer to our prayer is that God is our "shield and exceeding great reward" (Genesis 15:1). When that happens, all other desires, hopes, and dreams pale in comparison, and we find contentment fully and wholly in Him apart from obtaining the answers for which we pray.

I pray these simple helps will strengthen and undergird your waiting. May God reveal Himself to you as you wait patiently for the promises for which you are believing. In so doing, your roots will grow down deep into Him (Colossians 2:27).

For further meditation and application:

Which, if any, of the things mentioned in this chapter, have you found helpful in persevering in your prayers as you wait upon the Lord for an answer? Is there something you are not presently doing that the Holy Spirit is prompting you to do?

43

When All Else Fails, Let Jesus Pray

Consequently, he is able to save to the uttermost those who draw near to God through him, since he always lives to make intercession for them. Hebrews 7:25 ESV

Prayer in its purest and simplest form is not about what we say or how we say it. It is not about what we do or how we do it. To talk about praying effectively is to miss the point entirely. Prayer for the Christ follower is really more about *being* than *doing.* Its essence is discovered by being in a relationship with the one who is the lover of our soul and the friend who sticks closer than a brother (Proverbs 18:24).

Our human nature, in matters relating to God, almost always gravitates to doing rather than being. We feel responsible to do something to get God's attention or gain His favor. We are driven by a performance orientation that wants to prove to God our worth and our worthiness. That naturally carries over into our prayers.

But God's ways are higher than our ways, and our relationship with Him through His son Jesus Christ leaves

nothing for us to prove. Through Jesus' death, burial, and resurrection, He has already done it all. The uniqueness of the Christian faith compared to all the other religions of the world, both past and present, is that the word "done" has forever been substituted for the word "do".

As believers in Christ, most understand the *done* as it applies to our righteousness and salvation that comes through faith in what He did at the cross for the forgiveness of our sins. Without a doubt, that *done* is cause for the biggest sigh of relief and the greatest shout of joy we can utter.

Where we often struggle and revert back to *doing* is in our prayer lives. In Hebrews, we find a very insightful verse into the secret to struggle-free prayer. **"Consequently, he is able to save to the uttermost those who draw near to God through him, since he always lives to make intercession for them"** (Hebrews 7:25 ESV).

This verse emphasizes four things.
First, the work of Christ's salvation is an ongoing process in our lives, past, present, and future. Paul confirms this when he writes: *"**He has** rescued us from a terrible death, and **he will continue** to rescue us. Yes, he is the one on whom we have set our hope, and **he will rescue us again**"* (2 Corinthians 1:10 ISV *emphasis added*).

Second, Christ's salvation, which is to the "uttermost," has two dimensions. It literally means completely and forever. That is an all-encompassing statement, nothing is excluded, and no time limitations are placed upon it. In other words, no matter what trials come our way and no matter when they come, God promises to save us from them.

Third, the only requirement for this amazing promise to be fulfilled is for us to "draw near to God through him." It is an invitation to being in a close relationship with God the Father through Jesus Christ the Son – no *doing* required, just *being* in relationship.

Fourth, and this is the clincher, Jesus is committed to continually praying for us. The ultimate responsibility for prayer that gets answers is being shouldered by Him! This realization, that the burden and doing of prayer, just like our righteousness and salvation, are the responsibility of Jesus and not us, can revolutionize our prayer lives.

Job, whom we all know suffered unspeakable trials, had a similar and remarkable revelation in which he saw someone in the heavens interceding on his behalf. *"Even now my witness is in heaven; my advocate is on high. My intercessor is my friend* as my eyes pour out tears to God; on behalf of a man he pleads with God as a man pleads for his friend" (Job 16:19-21 NIV *emphasis added*). I believe this witness, advocate, and friend interceding on Job's behalf was Christ himself, the one who "always lives to make intercession." Such revelations are game changers when it comes to prayer.

At one critical point in my life, when I was laboring in prayer over an important issue, I just happened to stumble onto this verse. When I read it and realized that my closest lifelong friend, who is Jesus, the one who has always been with me and has never let me down, was praying for me, my heavy burden of doing prayer lifted. Faith and peace flooded my soul. I entered into an abiding place of rest in simply being in the presence of my intercessor, the one who was already doing the work of prayer on my behalf.

Jesus has promised that He would never leave us or forsake us, and that even if we find ourselves in hellish situations His Spirit would be there with us (Hebrews 11:5; Psalm 139:8). It is the Holy Spirit, sent from the Father as our comforter and counselor, who is ever present to help us in our weakness. For when "we do not know how to pray as we should. . . the Spirit Himself intercedes for us with groanings too deep for words" (Romans 8:26 NASB). When we are drained of words, when the pain, grief, and frustration are too overwhelming, we can derive great comfort in knowing that the Holy Spirit can take even our groans and sighs, and turn them into prayers.

When trials overwhelm us and accompanying fears and anxieties plague us, our natural tendency is to take the burden of prayer upon ourselves. Being assured that we are not alone, and that the burden of prayer is already being shouldered by Jesus through the power of the Holy Spirit, should release faith and peace.

For further meditation and application:

Has prayer become a *doing* drudgery for you? Perhaps it's an indication God is inviting you to concentrate more on *being* in His presence than *doing* prayer. What might that look like for you if you took some appropriate steps to remedy your situation?

About the Author

Tom Stuart is a member of the pastoral leadership team at the Twin Cities Justice House of Prayer (TCJHOP). He has a passion to raise up a praying and prevailing church that will answer Jesus' mandate to be a house of prayer for all nations. His call to prayer began early in his Christian life through an angelic visitation shortly after a Pauline conversion as a twenty-five year old agnostic post grad student. During that time God also sovereignly interrupted his pursuit of an architectural career and called him into a life of serving Him in the ministry.

His formative years were as a volunteer youth pastor, graduating eventually to a full time position at his home church of Way of the Cross. Over the course of time he became its associate pastor and then senior pastor. Out of that church he initiated a church planting effort that started four additional churches, including Bridgewood Community Church which the Lord led him to plant and pastor.

After nearly twenty years pastoring at Bridgewood, he transitioned the leadership to a next generation leader and became the Executive Director the Twin Cities House of Prayer in early 2014. He served in that capacity until mid-2015 when it merged with the Justice House of Prayer to become Twin Cities Justice House of Prayer.

He and his wife Susan have five children (all married) and ten grandchildren, and live near St. Paul, Minnesota. For more information about Tom's ministry and resources visit www.tomstuart.org.

Made in the USA
San Bernardino, CA
25 October 2015